Hugo's Simplified

Italian Phrase Book

Hugo's Language Books Limited

This edition

ISBN 0 85285 085 9

Compiled by
Lexus Ltd
with
Karen McAulay
and
Mariarosaria Cardines

Facts and figures given in this book were correct when printed. If you discover any changes, please write to us.

6th impression 1990

Set in 9/9 Plantin Light by
Typesetters Ltd and
printed in England by
Courier International Ltd,
Tiptree, Essex

CONTENTS

PREFACE

This is the latest in a long line of Hugo Phrase Books and is of excellent pedigree, having been compiled by experts to meet the general needs of tourists and business travellers. Arranged under the usual headings of 'Hotels', 'Motoring' and so forth, the ample selection of useful words and phrases is supported by an 1800-line mini-dictionary. By cross-reference to this, scores of additional phrases may be formed. There is also an extensive menu guide listing approximately 600 dishes or methods of cooking and presentation.

The pronunciation of words and phrases in the main text is imitated in English sound syllables, and highlighted sections illustrate some of the replies you may be given and the signs or instructions you may see and hear.

PRONUNCIATION

When reading the imitated pronunciation, stress that part which is underlined. Pronounce each syllable as if it formed part of an English word, and you will be understood sufficiently well. Remember the points below, and your pronunciation will be even closer to the correct Italian. Use our audio cassette of selected extracts from this book, and you should be word-perfect!

ai and *ay:*	to rhyme with 'fair'
r:	is always strongly pronounced
eh:	as in 'bed'
oh:	as in 'for'

Note that two identical consonants separated by a hyphen (vor-ray) indicate an elongated consonant, i.e. one which must be pronounced longer than the ordinary sound.

USEFUL EVERYDAY PHRASES

Yes/No
Sì/No
See/No

Thank you
Grazie
Gratzee-ay

No thank you
No grazie
No gratzee-ay

Please
Per favore, per piacere
Pair favvoreh, pair pee-achaireh

I don't understand
Non capisco
Non kapeesko

Do you speak English/French/Spanish?
Parla inglese/francese/spagnolo?
Parla eenglaizeh/franchaizeh/span-yollo?

I can't speak Italian
Non parlo italiano
Non parlo eetal-yanno

Please speak more slowly
Per favore, parli più lentamente
Pair favvoreh, parlee pyoo lentamenteh

Please write it down for me
Lo scriva, per favore
Loh skreeva, pair favvoreh

Good morning/good afternoon/good night
Buon giorno/buona sera/buona notte
Bwon jorno/bwona saira/bwona not-teh

Hello!
Ciao
Chow

Goodbye
Arrivederci/Arrivederla
Ar-reevedairchee/Ar-reevedairla

How are you?
Come sta/stai?
Komeh sta/sty?

Excuse me (may I get by?)
Permesso
Pairmesso

Sorry! (I beg your pardon)
Mi scusi!
Mee skoozee!

I'm really sorry
Sono spiacente
Sono spee-achenteh

I beg your pardon?
Prego?
Praygo?

Can you help me?
Può aiutarmi?
Pwo ayootarmee?

Can you tell me...?
Potrebbe dirmi...?
Potraib-beh deermee...?

Where is the lavatory please?
Per cortesia, dove sono i servizi?
Pair kortaizee-a, doveh sono ee sairveetzee?

Can I have...?
Potrei avere...?
Potray avaireh...?

I would like...
Vorrei...
Vor-ray...

Is there ... here?
C'è...?
Cheh...?

Where can I get...?
Dove potrei trovare...?
Doveh potray trovarreh...?

How much is it?
Quanto costa?
Kwannto kosta?

What time is it?
Che ore sono?
Kay oreh sono?

I must go now
Devo andare ora
Daivo andarreh ora

Cheers!
Alla salute!/Cin! Cin!
Al-la salooteh!/Cheen! Cheen!

Go away!
Mi lasci stare!/Va via!
Mee lashee starreh!/Va vee-a!

THINGS YOU'LL SEE OR HEAR

adulti	adults
aperto	open
arrivo	arrival
attenzione!	attention, caution
auguri!	good luck!, all the best!
bambini	children
cassa	till, cash desk
chiuso	closed
dentro	inside
destra	right
di sopra	upstairs
di sotto	downstairs
entrare	to enter
entrata	way in
fumatori	smokers
fuori	outside
fuori servizio	out of order
gabinetto	lavatory
grazie	thank you
ingresso	entrance

libero	vacant, free
mi scusi!	excuse me!
non fumatori	non-smokers
occupato	engaged
ore d'apertura	opening hours
partenza	departure
pedoni	pedestrians
per favore/per piacere	please
pericolo	danger
permesso	excuse me *(getting past)*
prego	you're welcome, after you, don't mention it *(after thanks)*
prenotato/riservato	reserved
signore	ladies
signori	gentlemen
sinistra	left
spingere	push
tirare	pull
uscita	way out
va bene	okay
vietato	do not...
vietato fumare	no smoking
vietato l'ingresso	no admission

DAYS, MONTHS, SEASONS

Sunday	domenica	*domeneeka*
Monday	lunedì	*loonedee*
Tuesday	martedì	*martedee*
Wednesday	mercoledì	*merkolledee*
Thursday	giovedì	*jovedee*
Friday	venerdì	*venerdee*
Saturday	sabato	*sabatto*
January	gennaio	*jen-na-yo*
February	febbraio	*feb-bra-yo*
March	marzo	*martzo*
April	aprile	*apreeleh*
May	maggio	*maj-jo*
June	giugno	*joon-yo*
July	luglio	*lool-yo*
August	agosto	*agosto*
September	settembre	*set-tembreh*
October	ottobre	*ot-tobreh*
November	novembre	*novembreh*
December	dicembre	*deechembreh*
Spring	primavera	*preemavaira*
Summer	estate	*estatteh*
Autumn	autunno	*outoon-no*
Winter	inverno	*eenvairno*
Christmas	Natale	*nattalleh*
Christmas Eve	la Vigilia di Natale	*veejeel-ya dee nattalleh*
Good Friday	Venerdì Santo	*venairdee santo*
Easter	Pasqua	*paskwah*
New Year	Capo d'Anno	*kappo dan-no*
New Year's Eve	San Silvestro	*san seelvestro*
Whitsun	Pentecoste	*pentekosteh*

NUMBERS

0 zero *tzairo*
1 uno *oono*
2 due *doo-eh*
3 tre *treh*
4 quattro *kwat-tro*
5 cinque *cheenkweh*
6 sei *say*
7 sette *set-teh*
8 otto *ot-to*
9 nove *novveh*
10 dieci *dee-aichee*
11 undici *oon-deechee*
12 dodici *doh-deechee*
13 tredici *tray-deechee*
14 quattordici *kwat-tor-deechee*
15 quindici *kween-deechee*
16 sedici *say-deechee*
17 diciassette *deechas-set-teh*
18 diciotto *deechot-to*
19 diciannove *deechan-novveh*
20 venti *ventee*
21 ventuno *vent-oono*
22 ventidue *ventee-doo-eh*
30 trenta *trenta*
40 quaranta *kwarranta*
50 cinquanta *cheenkwannta*
60 sessanta *ses-santa*
70 settanta *set-tanta*
80 ottanta *ot-tanta*
90 novanta *novvanta*
100 cento *chento*
110 centodieci *chento-dee-aichee*
200 duecento *doo-eh-chento*
1000 mille *meeleh*
1,000,000 un milione *oon meel-yoneh*

TIME

today	oggi	*oj-jee*
yesterday	ieri	*yairee*
tomorrow	domani	*domannee*
the day before yesterday	l'altro ieri	*laltro yairee*
the day after tomorrow	dopodomani	*dopodomannee*
this week	questa settimana	*kwesta set-teemana*
last week	la settimana scorsa	*la set-teemana skorsa*
next week	la settimana prossima	*la set-teemana prosseema*
this morning	stamattina	*stamat-teena*
this afternoon	questo pomeriggio	*kwesto pomereej-jo*
this evening	sta sera	*sta saira*
tonight	sta notte	*sta not-teh*
yesterday afternoon	ieri pomeriggio	*yairee pomereej-jo*
last night	ieri sera/notte	*yairee saira/not-teh*
tomorrow morning	domani mattina	*domannee mat-teena*
tomorrow night	domani sera	*domannee saira*
in three days	tra tre giorni	*tra treh jornee*
three days ago	tre giorni fa	*treh jornee fa*
late	tardi	*tardee*
early	presto	*presto*
soon	presto	*presto*
later on	più tardi	*pyoo tardee*
at the moment	in questo momento	*een kwesto momento*
second	un secondo	*sekondo*
minute	un minuto	*meenooto*
ten minutes	dieci minuti	*dee-aichee meenootee*
quarter of an hour	un quarto d'ora	*kwarrto dora*
half an hour	una mezz'ora	*medzora*
three quarters of an hour	tre quarti d'ora	*treh kwarrtee dora*

hour	un'ora	*ara*
day	un giorno	*jorno*
week	una settimana	*set-teemana*
fortnight, two weeks	quindici giorni	*kween-deechee jornee*
month	un mese	*maizeh*
year	un'anno	*an-no*

TELLING THE TIME

The 24 hour clock is used much more commonly than in Britain or the USA, both in the written form as in timetables, and verbally as in enquiry offices and when making appointments.

one o'clock	l'una	*loona*
ten past one	l'una e dieci	*loona ay dee-aichee*
quarter past one	l'una e un quarto	*loona ay oon kwarrto*
twenty past one	l'una e venti	*loona ay ventee*
half past one	l'una e mezza	*loona ay medza*
twenty to two	le due meno venti	*lay doo-eh maino ventee*
quarter to two	le due meno un quarto	*lay doo-eh maino oon kwarrto*
ten to two	le due meno dieci	*lay doo-eh maino dee-aichee*
two o'clock	le due	*lay doo-eh*
13.00 (1 pm)	le tredici	*lay tray-deechee*
16.30 (4.30 pm)	le sedici e trenta	*lay say-deechee ay trenta*
20.10 (8.10 pm)	le venti e dieci	*lay ventee ay dee-aichee*
at half past five	alle cinque e mezza	*al-leh cheenkweh ay medza*
at seven o'clock	alle sette	*al-leh set-teh*
noon	mezzogiorno	*medzojorno*
midnight	mezzanotte	*medzanot-teh*

HOTELS

Hotels in Italy have five classifications: de luxe, first, second, third and fourth. In addition, there are three categories of *pensione* (the first being on a par with 2nd class hotels as regards price), the more humble *locanda* or inn, and motels. Bear in mind that various service charges and taxes may be imposed, even though these may not be included in the quoted price. The Italian tourist organisation, E.N.I.T., publishes an annual directory of Italian hotels with up-to-date details of maximum and minimum prices and facilities.
If you arrive in a town without having booked previously, go directly to the *Azienda di Soggiorno e Turismo* (the Tourist Information Office) for help. Leaflets will be available in English and usually at least one person there will speak good English.
Hotel breakfast usually consists of brioches (a type of croissant) and coffee, but some hotels may provide an English breakfast on request. If you prefer self-catering, you can rent furnished flats in most holiday resorts. Book well in advance as many Italians also prefer this option.
If you are in transit and have to break your journey, most main train stations have *centri diurni* (daytime centres) which provide baths, toilets, restrooms, hairdressers, bars etc. These are open from 6am till midnight.

USEFUL WORDS AND PHRASES

balcony	il balcone	*bal-koneh*
bathroom	il bagno	*ban-yo*
bed	il letto	*let-to*
bedroom	la camera da letto	*kamera da let-to*
bill	il conto	*konto*
breakfast	la prima colazione	*preema kollatzioneh*
dining room	la sala da pranzo	*salla da prantzo*

dinner	la cena	*chaina*
double room	la camera doppia	*kamera dopee-a*
foyer	la hall	*ohl*
full board	la pensione completa	*pensee-oneh kompletta*
half board	la mezza pensione	*medza pensee-oneh*
hotel	l'hotel	*loh-tel*
key	la chiave	*kya-veh*
lift, elevator	l'ascensore	*lashen-soreh*
lounge	il salone	*salloneh*
lunch	il pranzo	*prantzo*
manager	il direttore	*deeret-toreh*
receipt	la ricevuta	*reechevoota*
reception	la reception	*'reception'*
receptionist	il/la receptionist	*'receptionist'*
restaurant	il ristorante	*reestoranteh*
room	la stanza	*stantza*
room service	il servizio in camera	*serveetzi-o een kamera*
shower	la doccia	*docha*
single room	la camera singola	*kamera seengola*
toilet	la toilette	*twallet*
twin room	la camera per due	*kamera per doo-eh*

Have you any vacancies?
Avete una stanza?
Avaiteh oona stantza?

I have a reservation
Ho prenotato una stanza
Oh prainotatto oona stantza

I'd like a single/double/twin room
Vorrei una stanza singola/doppia/con due letti
Vor-ray oona stantza seengola/dopee-a/kon doo-eh let-ti

I'd like a room with a bathroom/balcony
Vorrei una stanza con bagno/con il balcone
Vor-ray oona stantza kon ban-yo/con eel bal-koneh

I'd like a room for one night/three nights...
Vorrei una stanza per una notte/tre notti...
Vor-ray oona stantza pair oona not-teh/treh not-tee...

What is the charge per night?
Quant'è per notte?
Kwannteh pair not-teh?

REPLIES YOU MAY HEAR:

Mi spiace, siamo al completo
I'm sorry, we're full

Non ci sono più camere doppie
We have no double rooms left

Pagamento in anticipo
Please pay in advance

I don't know yet how long I'll stay
Non so ancora quanto tempo rimarrò
Non so ankora kwannto tempo reemarro

When is breakfast/lunch/dinner?
À che ora viene servito la prima colazione/il pranzo/la cena?
Ah kay ora vyenneh serveeto la preema kollatzioneh/eel prantzo/la chaina?

Would you have my luggage brought up?
Mi fa portare i bagagli in camera?
Mee fa portarreh ee bagall-yee een kamera?

Please call me at ... o'clock
Mi svegli, per favore, alle...
Mee zvail-yee, pair favvoreh, al-leh...

Can I have breakfast in my room?
Potrei avere la colazione in camera?
Potray avaireh la kollatzioneh een kamera?

I'll be back at ... o'clock
Tornerò alle...
Tornairo al-leh...

My room number is...
Il mio numero di stanza è...
Eel mee-o noomero dee stantza eh...

I'm leaving tomorrow
Parto domani
Parto domannee

Can I have the bill please?
Mi da il conto per favore?
Mee da eel konto pair favvoreh?

Can you recommend another hotel?
Potrebbe consigliarmi un altro hotel?
Potraib-beh konseel-yarmee oon ahltro oh-tel?

Can you get me a taxi?
Potrebbe chiamarmi un taxi per favore?
Potraib-beh kyamarmee oon taxee pair favvoreh?

THINGS YOU'LL SEE OR HEAR

ascensore	lift, elevator
bagno	bathroom
camera con prima colazione	bed and breakfast
camera doppia	double room
camera singola	single room
cena	dinner
colazione	breakfast
completo	no vacancies
conto	bill
doccia	shower
mezza pensione	half board
pensione completa	full board
pianterreno	ground floor
pranzo	lunch
prenotazione	reservation
reception	reception
ristorante	restaurant
spingere	push
stanza per due	twin room
toilette	toilet
uscita d'emergenza	emergency exit

CAMPING AND CARAVANNING

Camping sites in Italy usually have excellent facilities. Prices differ according to the size of tent (*casetta* = "little house"; *canadese* = two man tent), and/or the number of people sharing it. You can generally pay for a space for the car next to the tent. Moving the car at certain times (e.g. mealtimes) is forbidden as it raises dust. If you go out in the evening you will not be allowed to bring your car back inside the site after midnight, but there are often parking facilities just outside.

Most campsites have electricity generators, for the use of which a small daily fee will be added to your bill. Toilet and washing facilities are very good. For a hot shower you may have to pay L.200 - which you insert in a machine attached to the shower. If tokens (*gettoni*) are needed these will be obtainable at the campsite office. Cold showers are free. The campsite office usually acts as a mini-bank as well. You can deposit all your money there and withdraw it on a daily basis. The office will also exchange foreign currency.

USEFUL WORDS AND PHRASES

bucket	il secchio	*saik-yo*
campsite	il campeggio	*kampej-jo*
campfire	il fuoco da campo	*fwokko da kampo*
to go camping	andare in campeggio	*andarreh een kampej-jo*
caravan, R.V.	la roulotte	*roolot*
cooking utensils	gli utensili per cucina	*ootenseelee pair koocheena*
drinking water	l'acqua potabile	*lakkwa pota-beeleh*
ground sheet	il telone impermeabile	*telloneh eempair may-abeeleh*
to hitch-hike	fare l'autostop	*farreh louto-stop*
rope	la fune, corda	*fooneh, korda*
rubbish	l'immondizia	*leem-mondeetzee-a*
rucksack	lo zaino	*tza-eeno*

saucepans	le pentole	*pentolleh*
sleeping bag	il sacco a pelo	*sak-ko a pailo*
tent	la tenda	*tenda*
youth hostel	l'ostello della gioventù	*lostel-lo del-la joventoo*

Can I camp here?
Posso campeggiare qui?
Pos-so kampej-jarreh kwee?

Can we park the caravan (trailer) here?
Possiamo parcheggiare la roulotte qui?
Pos-see-ammo parkej-jarreh la roolot kwee?

Where is the nearest campsite/caravan site?
Qual'è il campeggio più vicino?
Kwalleh eel kampej-jo pyoo veecheeno?

What is the charge per night?
Quanto si paga per notte?
Kwannto see pagga pair not-teh?

What facilities are there?
Di quali servizi dispone?
Dee kwallee sairveet-zee deesponeh?

Can I light a fire here?
Posso accendere il fuoco qui?
Pos-so achendereh eel fwokko kwee?

Where can I get...?
Dove posso trovare...?
Doveh pos-so trovarreh...?

Is there drinking water here?
C'è acqua potabile?
Cheh akkwa pota-beeleh?

THINGS YOU'LL SEE OR HEAR

acqua potabile	drinking water
carta d'identità	pass, identity card
campeggio	campsite
coperta	blanket
cucina	kitchen
doccia	shower
fuoco	fire
luce	light
ostello della gioventù	Youth Hostel
picchetto (da tenda)	tent peg
prestare	to lend
rimorchio	trailer
roulotte	caravan, trailer (R.V.)
sacco a pelo	sleeping bag
tariffa	charge
tenda	tent
toilette, gabinetto	toilet
vietato campeggiare	no camping

MOTORING

Rules of the Road. In Italy you drive on the right and overtake on the left. On dual lane highways you may stay in the left-hand lane if heavy traffic has taken over the right-hand lane. Normally you may move from the right to the left-hand lane only for turning or overtaking. On three-lane roads with traffic flowing in both directions the central lane is for overtaking only.

At junctions where there are no indications or traffic lights, you must give way to traffic coming from the right, except in the case of a service station exit, a private road or a path entering the main road. Usually, a diamond-shaped yellow sign tells you that you have right of way; the end of this right of way is indicated by a similar sign with a bar through it. An upside-down red triangle or a 'STOP' sign indicates that you must give way to all vehicles coming both from the right and from the left.

In built-up areas the speed limit is 50kmh (31 mph). Official speed limits on open roads are more complex and depend on the cc of your car: up to 600cc the limit is 80kmh (50mph) with 90kmh (56mph) on motorways; from 600 to 900cc it's 90kmh (56mph) with 110kmh (69mph) on motorways; from 900 to 1300cc it's 100kmh (62mph) with 130kmh (81mph) on motorways; over 1300cc the limit is 110kmh (69mph) with 140kmh (87mph) on motorways.

If you have a breakdown and are forced to stop in the middle of the road, you must place a red triangle 50 metres behind your vehicle to warn other drivers. All drivers must carry this triangle - which can be rented from the offices of the ACI (Automobile Club Italiano) on entering Italy and then returned on leaving the country.

For emergency services dial 116 (or 01 in the provinces of Potenza, Catanzaro, Lecce or Caltanisetta) and you will be put in contact with the ACI who will provide immediate assistance. If the breakdown occurs on the Autostrada del Sole (Milan-Rome) there are emergency telephones on the right side of the motorway at intervals of 2kms. Motorists must NOT walk along the motorway if the breakdown occurs between two telephones but must ask a passing motorist for assistance.

SOME COMMON ROAD SIGNS

area riservata ai ciclisti	cyclists only
area riservata ai pedoni	pedestrians only
caduta massi	falling rocks
cunetta o dosso	ditch
dare precedenza	give way
discesa pericoloso	dangerous descent
disporsi in due file	two-lane traffic
divieto di accesso	no entry
divieto di segnalazioni acustiche	no horns
divieto di sorpasso	no overtaking
divieto di sosta	no parking
divieto di transito nei due sensi a tutti i veicoli	no vehicles
doppio senso di circolazione	two way traffic
incrocio	junction
lavori in corso	roadworks
passaggio a livello	level crossing
rallentare	slow down
senso unico	one way
strada con diritto di precedenza	road with right of way
strada ghiacciata	ice on road
strada sdrucciolevole	slippery road
strettoia	road narrows on both sides

USEFUL WORDS AND PHRASES

accelerator	l'acceleratore	*lachelairatoreh*
boot	il portabagagli	*portabagall-yee*
bonnet	il cofano	*koffano*
breakdown	il guasto	*gwasto*
brake	il freno	*fraino*
car	l'automobile, la macchina	*outomobeeleh, mak-keena*
car-body	la carrozzeria	*kar-rotzeree-a*
caravan	la roulotte	*roolot*
clutch	la frizione	*freetzioneh*
crossroads	l'incrocio	*leenkrocho*
to drive	guidare	*gweedarreh*
engine	il motore	*motoreh*
exhaust	lo scappamento	*skap-pamento*
exhaust pipe	il tubo di scappamento	*toobo dee skap-pamento*
fanbelt	la cinghia della ventola	*cheengya del-la ventola*
garage *(for repairs)*	l'autorimessa	*loutoreemes-sa*
(for fuel)	la stazione di servizio	*statzioneh dee sairveetzee-o*
gas(oline)	la benzina	*bendzeena*
gear	la marcia	*marcha*
hood	il cofano	*koffano*
ignition	l'accensione	*lachen-sioneh*
indicator	l'indicatore	*leendeekatoreh*
junction on motorway	il raccordo autostradale	*rak-kordo outo-stradalleh*
licence	la patente	*pattenteh*
lights *(head)*	i fari	*farree*
(rear)	i fari posteriori	*farree postairee-ohree*
lorry	il camion, l'autocarro	*kammion, loutokar-ro*
mirror	lo specchietto	*spek-kyetto*

motorbike	la motocicletta	*motocheekletta*
motorway	l'autostrada	*outostradda*
number plate	la targa	*targa*
oil	l'olio	*lol-yo*
petrol	la benzina	*bendzeena*
pump	la pompa	*pompa*
road	la strada	*stradda*
skid	slittare, sbandare	*zleetarreh, sbandarreh*
spares	i pezzi di ricambio	*petzee dee reekambee-o*
speed	la velocità	*vailocheeta*
speed limit	il limite di velocità	*leemeeteh dee vailocheeta*
speedometer	il tachimetro	*takkeemetro*
steering wheel	il volante	*volanteh*
tank	il serbatoio	*serbatto-yo*
tire/tyre	la gomma	*gohm-ma*
	il pneumatico	*pnayoomateeko*
tow	rimorchiare	*reemork-yarreh*
trailer	il rimorchio	*reemorkee-o*
trailer (R.V.)	la roulotte	*roolot*
truck	il camion, l'autocarro	*kammion, loutokar-ro*
trunk	il portabagagli	*portabagall-yee*
van	il furgone	*foorgoneh*
wheel	la ruota	*rwotta*
windscreen/shield	la parabrezza	*parabraitza*
windscreen wiper	il tergicristallo	*tairjee-kreestal-lo*

I'd like some fuel/oil/water
Mi dia della benzina/dell'olio/dell'acqua, per favore
Mee dee-a del-la bendzeena/del ol-yo/del akkwa, pair favvoreh

Fill her up please!
Faccia il pieno, per cortesia!
Facha eel pyaino, pair kortaizee-a!

I'd like 10 litres of fuel
Mi dia 10 litri di benzina, per favore
Mee dee-a dee-aichee leetree dee bendzeena, pair favvoreh

Would you check the tires (tyres) please?
Può controllare le gomme, per cortesia?
Pwo kontrol-larreh lay gohm-meh, pair kortaizee-a?

Where is the nearest filling station/garage?
Dov'è la stazione di servizio/autorimessa più vicina?
Doveh la statzioneh dee sairveetzi-oo/outoreemes-sa pyoo veecheena?

How do I get to...?
Può dirmi come andare a...?
Pwo deermee komeh andarreh ah...?

Is this the road to...?
È questa la strada per...?
Eh kwesta la stradda pair...?

DIRECTIONS YOU MAY BE GIVEN

dritto	straight on
a sinistra	left
giri a sinistra	turn left
a destra	right
giri a destra	turn right
il primo/la prima a destra	first on the right
il secondo/la seconda a sinistra	second on the left
vada oltre...	go past the...

Do you do repairs?
Lei effettua riparazioni?
Lay ef-fet-too-a reeparratzionee?

Can you repair the clutch?
Può ripararmi la frizione?
Pwo reeparrarmee la freetzioneh?

How long will it take?
Quanto tempo ci vorrà?
Kwannto tempo chee vor-rah?

There is something wrong with the engine
C'è qualcosa che non va con il motore
Cheh kwallkoza kay non va kon eel motoreh

The engine is overheating
Il motore si surriscalda
Eel motoreh see soor-reeskallda

The brakes are slipping
I freni non funzionano
Ee frainee non foontzion-ano

I need a new tire (tyre)
Ho bisogno di una gomma nuova
Oh beezon-yo dee oona gohm-ma nwova

Where can I hire a car?
Dove posso noleggiare una macchina?
Doveh pos-so nolej-jarreh oona mak-keena?

I'd like to hire a car
Vorrei noleggiare una macchina
Vor-ray nolej-jarreh oona mak-keena

Where can I park?
Dove posso parcheggiare?
Doveh pos-so parkej-jarreh?

Can I park here?
Posso parcheggiare qui?
Pos-so parkej-jarreh kwee?

THINGS YOU'LL SEE OR HEAR

autorimessa	garage *(for repairs)*
autostrada	motorway
cassello dell'autostrada	motorway toll booth
deviazione	diversion
fila (colonna) di macchine	traffic queue
ingorgo	traffic jam
livello dell'olio	oil level
normale	2 or 3 star fuel
pressione delle gomme	air pressure
olio	oil
raccordo autostradale	motorway junction
riparazione	repair
stazione di servizio	service and petrol station
strada statale	state highway
tergicristallo	windscreen/windshield wipers
uscita	exit

RAIL TRAVEL

Trains on Italian State Railways (F.S. = *Ferrovie dello Stato*) are classified as follows:
T.E.E. (Trans-European Express): very fast, first class only. A supplement is charged and advance booking is essential.
Rapido: Long-distance express train. Charges a supplement which even children must pay in full.
Espresso: Long-distance fast train. No supplement required.
Diretto: Long-distance train stopping at main stations.
Locale: Small local train stopping at main stations.

Travelling by train in the tourist season can be a nightmare so, wherever possible, book your seat well in advance.

Rail travel is so cheap and efficient in Italy that it is very widely used. Children under 4 years of age not occupying a seat travel free, and there is a half-price fare for children between 4 and 12 years. Considerable reductions are available for families and individuals on short term season tickets. Couchettes are available on most domestic long-distance night services and most long-distance trains have restaurant cars. On shorter journeys there will be a trolley on the train from which you can buy sandwiches and soft drinks. In main stations platform vendors pass by the train windows.

USEFUL WORDS AND PHRASES

booking office	la biglietteria, l'ufficio prenotazioni	*beel-yet-teree-a, loof-feecho prainotatzioneh*
buffet	il buffet	*boofay*
carriage, car	la carrozza, il vagone	*kar-rotza, vaggoneh*
compartment	lo scompartimento	*skomparteemento*
connection	la coincidenza	*ko-eencheedentza*

currency exchange	il cambio	*kambee-o*
dining car	il vagone ristorante	*vaggoneh reestoranteh*
emergency alarm	il segnale d'allarme, l'allarme	*sen-yalleh dal-larmeh,*
engine	la locomotiva	*lokomoteeva*
entrance	l'entrata	*lentratta*
exit	l'uscita	*looseheeta*
first class	la prima classe	*preema klas-seh*
to get in	salire	*salleereh*
to get out	scendere	*shendereh*
guard	il capotreno	*kappotraino*
indicator board	il tabellone	*tabbel-loneh*
left luggage	il deposito bagagli	*daipozeeto bagall-yee*
lost property	gli oggetti smarriti	*ojet-tee zmar-reettee*
luggage rack	la rete portabagagli	*raiteh portabagall-yee*
luggage trolley	il carrello	*kar-rel-lo*
luggage van	il bagagliaio	*bagall-ya-yo*
platform	il binario	*beenaree-o*
rail	la rotaia	*rota-ya*
railway	la ferrovia	*fer-rovee-a*
reserved seat	il posto riservato	*posto ree-sairvatto*
restaurant car	il vagone ristorante	*vaggoneh reestoranteh*
return ticket	il biglietto di andata e ritorno	*beel-yet-to dee andatta ay reetorno*
seat	il posto (a sedere)	*posto ah sedaireh*
second class	la seconda classe	*sekonda klas-seh*
single ticket	il biglietto di andata	*beel-yet-to dee andatta*
sleeping car	il vagone letto	*vaggoneh let-to*
station	la stazione	*statzioneh*
station master	il capostazione	*kappo-statzioneh*
ticket	il biglietto	*beel-yet-to*
ticket collector	il bigliettaio	*beel-yet-ta-yo*
timetable	l'orario	*lorarree-o*
tracks	i binari	*beenaree*
train	il treno	*traino*
waiting room	la sala d'attesa	*salla dat-taiza*
window	il finestrino	*feenestreeno*

When does the train for ... leave?
À che ora parte il treno per...?
Ah kay ora parteh eel traino pair...?

When does the train from ... arrive?
À che ora arriva il treno da...?
Ah kay ora ar-reeva eel traino da...?

When is the next/first/last train to...?
À che ora c'è il prossimo/primo/l'ultimo treno per...?
Ah kay ora cheh eel pros-seemo/preemo/loolteemo traino pair...?

Do I have to change?
Devo cambiare?
Daivo kambee-arreh?

What is the fare to...?
Quanto costa il biglietto per...?
Kwannto kosta eel beel-yet-to pair...?

A single/return ticket to ... please
Un biglietto di andata/di andata e ritorno per ..., per favore
Oon beel-yet-to dee andatta/dee andatta ay reetorno pair ..., pair favvoreh

Do I have to pay a supplement?
Devo pagare il supplemento?
Daivo paggarreh eel sooplaimento?

I'd like to reserve a seat
Vorrei prenotare un posto a sedere
Vor-ray prainotarreh oon posto ah sedaireh

Does the train stop at...?
Ferma il treno a...?
Fairma eel traino ah...?

How long does it take to get to...?
Quanto tempo ci s'impiega per andare a...?
Kwannto tempo chee seemp-yaiga pair andarreh ah...?

REPLIES YOU MAY BE GIVEN

Il prossimo treno parte alle...
The next train is at...

Deve cambiare a...
Change at...

C'è solo la prima classe
There is only 1st class

Deve pagare un supplemento
You must pay a supplement.

Is this the right train for...?
È questo il treno per...?
Eh kwesto eel traino pair...?

Is this the right platform for the ... train?
È questo il binario del treno per...?
Eh kwesto eel beenaree-o del traino pair...?

At which platform does the train for ... arrive?
Su che binario arriva il treno per...?
Soo kay beenaree-o ar-reeva eel traino pair...?

From which platform does the train for ... leave?
Da che binario parte il treno per...?
Da kay beenaree-o parteh eel traino pair...?

Is the train late?
È in ritardo il treno?
Eh een reetardo eel traino?

Could you help me with my luggage please?
Potrebbe darmi una mano con i bagagli?
Potraib-beh darrmee oona manno kon ee bagall-yee?

Is this a non-smoking compartment?
È uno scompartimento non fumatori?
Eh oono skomparteemento non foomatoree?

Is this seat free?
È libero questo posto?
Eh leebairo kwesto posto?

This seat is taken
Questo posto è occupato
Kwesto posto eh ok-koopatto

I have reserved this seat
Questo posto è riservato
Kwesto posto eh ree-sairvatto

May I open/close the window?
Posso aprire/chiudere il finestrino?
Pos-so appreereh/kyoodereh eel feenestreeno?

When do we arrive in...?
À che ora arriviamo a...?
Ah kay ora arriviamo a...?

What station is this?
Che stazione è questa?
Kay statzioneh eh kwesta?

When does my connection leave...?
À che ora c'è la coincidenza per...?
Ah kay ora cheh la ko-eencheedentza pair...?

Do we stop at...?
Ci fermiamo a...?
Chee fairmee-ammo ah...?

Would you keep an eye on my things for a moment?
Le dispiace dare per un momento uno sguardo alla mia roba?
Lay deespee-acheh darreh per oon momento oono zgwarrdo al-la mee-a robba?

Is there a restaurant car on this train?
C'è un vagone ristorante su questo treno?
Cheh oon vaggoneh reestoranteh soo kwesto traino?

THINGS YOU'LL SEE OR HEAR

ai binari	to the platforms
ai treni	to the trains
arrivi	arrivals
attenzione	attention
biglietto	ticket
biglietto d'accesso	platform ticket
cambio	exchange
carrozza	carriage, car
cuccetta	sleeping car
deposito bagagli	left luggage
diretto	long-distance train
distributore automatico di biglietti	ticket machine
entrata	way in, entrance
è pericoloso sporgersi	it is dangerous to lean out
espresso	long-distance fast train

il sabato	Saturdays
informazioni	information
la domenica	Sundays
la domenica e i giorni festivi	Sundays and holidays
libero	free
...minuti/ore in ritardo	...minutes/hours late
non ferma a...	does not stop at...
occupato	engaged, reserved
oggetti smarriti	lost property
ogni abuso sarà punito con...	penalty for misuse...
orario	timetable
partenze	departures
prenotazione posto a sedere	reserved seat
pronto soccorso	first aid, casualty
rapido	fast train
ritardo	delay
riservato	reserved
riservato ai non fumatori	non-smokers only
sala d'attesa	waiting room
salire su	to get on
scendere da	to get off
solo il/la...	...-days only
spuntini, panini	snacks, sandwiches
supplemento rapido	supplementary fare for fast train
(segnale d')allarme	emergency alarm
toilette	toilet, lavatory
vagone	carriage, car
vagone letto	sleeping car
vagone ristorante	restaurant car
viaggio	journey
vietato fumare	no smoking
vietato l'ingressso	no entry
vietato sporgersi	do not lean out

AIR TRAVEL

USEFUL WORDS AND PHRASES

aircraft	l'aereo	*la-airay-o*
air hostess	la hostess di volo	*ostess dee vollo*
airline	la linea aerea	*leenay-a ah-airay-a*
airport	l'aeroporto	*la-airoporto*
airport bus	l'autobus per l'aeroporto	*lout-oboos pair la-airoporto*
arrival	l'arrivo	*lar-reevo*
baggage claim	il ritiro bagagli	*reeteero bagall-yee*
boarding card	la carta d'imbarco	*karta deembarko*
check-in	il check-in	*'check-in'*
check-in desk	l'accettazione (bagagli)	*lachet-tatzioneh (bagall-yee)*
delay	il ritardo	*reetardo*
departure	la partenza	*partentza*
departure lounge	la sala d'attesa	*salla dat-taiza*
emergency exit	l'uscita di sicurezza	*loosheeta dee seekooretza*
flight	il volo	*vollo*
flight number	il numero del volo	*noomero dell vollo*
gate	l'uscita	*loosheeta*
land	atterrare	*at-tair-rarreh*
passport	il passaporto	*pas-saporto*
passport control	il controlla passaporti	*kontrol-lo pas-saportee*
pilot	il pilota	*peelotta*
runway	la pista	*peesta*
seat	il posto	*posto*
seat belt	la cintura di sicurezza	*cheentura dee seekooretza*
steward	lo steward	*'steward'*
stewardess	la hostess	*ostess*
take off	decollare	*daikol-larreh*
window	il finestrino	*feenestreeno*
wing	l'ala	*lalla*

When is there a flight to...?
À che ora c'è un aereo per...?
Ah kay ora cheh oon ah-airay-o pair...?

What time does the flight to ... leave?
À che ora parte l'aereo per...?
Ah kay ora parteh la-airay-o pair...?

Is it a direct flight?
È un volo diretto?
Eh oon vollo deeret-to?

Do I have to change planes?
Devo cambiare aereo?
Daivo kambee-arreh ah-airay-o?

When do I have to check in?
À che ora devo fare il check-in?
Ah kay ora daivo farreh eel check-in?

I'd like a single/return ticket to...
Vorrei un biglietto di andata/andata e ritorno per...
Vor-ray oon beel-yet-to dee andatta/andatta ay reetorno pair...

I'd like a non-smoking seat please
Vorrei un posto riservato ai non fumatori
Vor-ray oon posto ree-servatto eye non foomatoree

I'd like a window seat please
Vorrei un posto vicino al finestrino
Vor-ray oon posto veecheeno al feenestreeno

How long will the flight be delayed?
Con quanto ritardo partirà l'aereo?
Kon kwannto reetardo parteera la-airay-o?

Is this the right gate for the...flight?
È questa l'uscita del volo per...?
Eh kwesta loosheeta del vollo pair...?

When do we arrive in...?
À che ora arriveremo a...?
Ah kay ora ar-reevairay-mo ah...?

May I smoke now?
Posso fumare ora?
Pos-so foomarreh ora?

I do not feel very well
Non mi sento molto bene
Non mee sento molto beneh

THINGS YOU'LL SEE OR HEAR

accettazione (bagagli)	check-in desk
aereo	aeroplane
allacciare le cinture di sicurezza	fasten your safety belts
altitudine	altitude
arrivo	arrival
atterraggio	landing
atterraggio d'emergenza	emergency landing
capitano	captain
check-in	check-in
controllo bagagli	baggage control
controllo passaporti	passport control
decollo	take off
equippaggio	crew
fare il check-in	to check in
fumatori	smokers
hostess	stewardess
informazioni	information
non fumatori	non-smokers
ora locale	local time
orario di volo	flight time
partenza	departure
passeggeri	passengers
pista	runway
pronti per il decollo	ready for take-off
ritiro bagagli	baggage claim
scala, scaletta, scalo	steps
uscita	exit
uscita di sicurezza	emergency exit
velocità	speed
vietato fumare	no smoking
volo	flight
volo di linea	scheduled flight
volo diretto	direct flight

LOCAL PUBLIC TRANSPORT

In large cities there are several types of public transport: bus, trolle bus (*filovia*), tram or streetcar, and underground or subwa (*Metropolitana*). In some cities there is an integrated public transpo system, which means that the same tickets can be used on every typ of transport. Tickets are cheap, operate on a flat-fare basis and a valid for 60 to 75 minutes, depending on the city. Tickets can b bought in the underground, at any newspaper kiosk, *tabaccaio* c ordinary bar with a 'VENDITA BIGLIETTI' sign in the windov When you enter a bus, *filovia* etc (entry by the rear door) you mus insert your ticket in a machine which stamps the time on it. Th only restriction on use of the ticket is that you cannot re-enter th *Metropolitana* with the same ticket, even if you have not yet use up your 75 minutes. There are inspectors who make random check and if you are travelling irregularly you can then expect an on-th spot fine of approx. L.20,000. In most places public transport is ver quick and efficient. Smoking is forbidden.

In Venice (where of course there are no buses etc) you travel b *vaporetto*, a small passenger boat, paying the fare when you boarc Here, the rate is according to the distance you wish to travel. Ther are, however, special offers, such as cheap 24-hour tickets with whic you can travel on any number of boats for any distance, starting fror the time when you stamp your ticket at the boat stop (not from whe you buy it).

People rarely travel long distances by coach in Italy as the rail servic is so cheap and efficient. Local coaches for small towns and place of interest are generally inexpensive and the service frequent. Th coaches often have a system similar to that of the buses: when yo enter (rear entry) you stamp your ticket in the ticket-stamping machin

Taxis in Italy are yellow. It is inadvisable to ride in any taxi whic is not yellow. These are private taxis and may charge astronomic prices. Yellow taxis are reliable and efficient but they do have a hig minimum charge so it is uneconomical to use them for very sho distances. If you have a lot of luggage, then there may be an extr charge.

USEFUL WORDS AND PHRASES

adult	l'adulto	*ladoolto*
boat	la barca, l'imbarcazione	*barka, leembarkatzioneh*
bus	l'autobus	*lout-oboos*
bus stop	la fermata dell'autobus	*fermatta del lout-oboos*
child	il bambino, la bambina	*bam-beeno, bam-beena*
coach	la corriera, il pullman	*kor-ree-aira, poolman*
conductor	il bigliettaio	*beel-yet-ta-yo*
connection	la coincidenza	*ko-eencheedentza*
cruise	la crociera	*krochaira*
driver	l'autista	*louteesta*
fare	il biglietto	*beel-yet-to*
ferry	il traghetto	*trag-et-to*
lake	il lago	*laggo*
network map	la pianta dei trasporti pubblici	*pee-anta day trasportee poobleechee*
number ... bus	l'autobus numero ...	*lout-oboos noomero ...*
passenger	il passeggero	*passej-jairo*
port	il porto	*porto*
quay	il molo	*molo*
river	il fiume	*fyoomeh*
sea	il mare	*marreh*
seat	il posto	*posto*
ship	la nave	*navveh*
station	la stazione	*statzioneh*
taxi	il taxi	*'taxi'*
terminus	il capolinea	*kappoleenay-a*
ticket	il biglietto	*beel-yet-to*
tram, streetcar	il tram	*tram*
tram stop	la fermata del tram	*fermatta del tram*
underground, subway	la metropolitana	*metro-polleeta-na*

Where is the nearest underground station?
Qual'è la stazione della metropolitana più vicina?
Kwalleh la statzioneh del-la metro-polleeta-na pyoo veecheena?

Where is the bus station?
Dov'è la stazione delle autolinee?
Doveh la statzioneh del-leh outoleeneh-eh?

Where is there a bus stop/tram stop?
Dov'è la fermata dell'autobus/del tram?
Doveh la fermatta del lout-oboos/del tram?

Which buses go to...?
Quale autobus va a...?
Kwalleh out-oboos va a...?

How often do the buses/trams to ... run?
Ogni quanto passa l'autobus/il tram per...?
Onn-yee kwannto pas-sa lout-oboos/eel tram pair...?

Would you tell me when we get to...?
Potrebbe dirmi quando arriviamo a...?
Potraib-beh deermee kwanndo ar-reevee-ammo ah...?

Do I have to get off yet?
Devo scendere qui?
Daivo shendereh kwee?

How do you get to...?
Como posso andare a...?
Komeh pos-so andarreh ah...?

Is it very far?
È lontano?
Eh lontanno?

I want to go to...
Voglio andare a...
Voll-yo andarreh ah...

Do you go near...?
Lei passa vicino...?
Lay pas-sa veecheeno...?

Where can I buy a ticket?
Dove posso comprare il biglietto?
Doveh pos-so komprarreh eel beel-yet-to?

Please close/open the window
Apra/chiude il finestrino, per piacere
Appra/kyoodeh eel feenestreeno, pair pee-achaireh.

Could you help me get a ticket?
Potrebbe aiutarmi a comprare il biglietto?
Potraib-beh ayootarmee a komprarreh eel beel-yet-to?

When does the last bus leave?
À che ora parte l'ultimo autobus?
Ah kay ora parteh loolteemo out-oboos?

Where can I get a taxi from?
Dove posso prendere un taxi?
Doveh pos-so prendereh oon taxee.

Please stop here
Si fermi qui, per favore
See fairmee kwee, pair favvoreh

I'd like a receipt please
Vorrei la ricevuta, per favore
Vor-ray la reechevoota, pair favvoreh

THINGS YOU'LL SEE OR HEAR

abbonamento mensile	monthly ticket
abbonamento settimanale	weekly ticket
adulti	adults
autista	driver
bambini	children
biglietto	ticket
biglietto giornaliero	day ticket
cambiare	to change
capolinea	terminus
controllo biglietti	ticket inspection
controllare	to check, inspect
discesa	exit
distributore automatico di biglietti	ticket machine
fermata	stop
giro in barca	boat trip
il porto	harbour, port
linea	route
macchina obliteratrice	stamping machine
mostrare	to show
pagare	to pay
partenza	departure
passeggero sprovvisto di biglietto	fare dodger
posti in piedi	standing room
posto (a sedere)	seat
salita	entry
tessera di libera circolazione	multi-journey ticket
tesserino	travelcard
tragitto breve	short journey
uscita di sicurezza	emergency exit
vietato fumare	no smoking
vietato l'ingresso	no entry

RESTAURANT

There are various types of places for eating out. For snacks the most common is the bar. These are open continuously from early morning until about 10pm. They are all licensed to sell alcohol and usually offer a variety of sandwiches, rolls, cakes and hot and cold drinks. In most bars you are required to go first to the cash desk, make your order, pay and get a receipt *(scontrino)* which you then hand to the barman and repeat your order. (Tourists are very often unaware of this special procedure.) You will notice that most Italians stand up in bars - sitting down costs extra. The sign 'Tavola Calda' means that hot dishes are also served.

For full meals there is the *locanda*, *osteria*, *pizzeria*, *trattoria*, *taverna* and *ristorante*. Wherever possible, it's a good idea to choose the tourist menu (*menu turistico*) or the set menu (*menu fisso*). Although the variety is more restricted, the food is of the same standard and you get a good deal more for your money, without having to face any service charge shocks at the end of the meal. Always ask for the local culinary specialities and local wine as they are generally excellent, and wine is a great deal cheaper and of superior quality in its place of origin.

USEFUL WORDS AND PHRASES

Here is a list of the basic words you'll need; you'll find an extremely comprehensive menu guide at the end of this section.

beer	la birra	*beer-ra*
bill	il conto	*konto*
bottle	la bottiglia	*bot-teel-ya*
bowl	la scodella	*skodel-la*
cake	la torta	*torta*
chef	il cuoco	*kwokko*
	la cuoca	*kwokka*
coffee	il caffè	*kaffeh*

cup	la tazza	*tatza*
glass	il bicchiere	*beek-yaireh*
fork	la forchetta	*forket-ta*
knife	il coltello	*koltel-lo*
meal	il pasto	*pas-to*
menu	il menu	*minnoo*
milk	il latte	*lat-teh*
plate	il piatto	*pyat-to*
receipt	la ricevuta	*reechevoota*
sandwich	il panino	*pan-eeno*
serviette	il tovagliolo	*toval-yollo*
snack	lo spuntino	*spoonteeno*
soup	la minestra	*meenestra*
spoon	il cucchiaio	*kook-ya-yo*
sugar	lo zucchero	*dzookairo*
table	il tavolo	*tavvolo*
teaspoon	il cucchiaino	*kook-ya-eeno*
tip	la mancia	*mancha*
waiter	il cameriere	*kammer-yaireh*
waitress	la cameriera	*kammer-yaira*
water	l'acqua	*lakkwa*
wine	il vino	*veeno*
wine list	la lista dei vini	*leesta day veenee*

A table for 1/2/3 please
Un tavolo per una persona/per due/per tre, per favore
Oon tavvolo pair oona pairssona/pair doo-eh/pair treh, pair favvoreh

Can we see the menu/wine list?
Potrebbe darci il menu/la lista dei vini?
Potraib-be darchee eel minnoo/la leesta day veenee?

What would you recommend?
Cosa ci consiglia?
Koza chee konseel-ya?

Can we have a local wine?
Potremmo assaggiare un vino locale?
Potraim-mo as-saj-jarreh oon veeno lokalleh?

Can we try a local speciality?
Potremmo assaggiare una specialità locale?
Potraim-mo as-saj-jarreh oona spechaleeta lokalleh?

I'd like...
Vorrei...
Vor-ray...

We only want a snack
Vorremmo fare solo uno spuntino
Vor-raimo farreh solo oono spoonteeno

We just want a cup of coffee/tea
Vogliamo solo una tazza di caffè/di tè
Voll-yammo solo oona tatza dee kaffeh/dee tay

Is there a set menu?
C'è un menu fisso?
Cheh oon minnoo fees-so?

Waiter!
Cameriere!
Kammer-yaireh!

We didn't order this!
Non lo abbiamo ordinato!
Non loh ab-bee-ammo ordeenatto!

Can we have the bill please?
Può portarci il conto, per favore?
Pwo portarchee eel konto, pair favvoreh?

I'd like a receipt please
Vorrei la ricevuta, per favore
Vor-ray la reechevoota, pair favvoreh

I think there's a mistake in the bill
Credo chi ci sia un errore nel conto
Kraido kay chee see-a oon er-roreh nel konto

The meal was very good, thank you
La cena è stata ottima
La chaina eh statta ot-teema

My compliments to the chef!
Faccio i miei complimenti al cuoco!
Facho ee mee-ayee kompleementee al kwokko!

MENU GUIDE

abbacchio alla romana	spring lamb Roman style
acciughe sott'olio	anchovies in oil
aceto	vinegar
acqua	water
acqua minerale gassata	sparkling mineral water
acqua minerale non gassata	still mineral water
acqua naturale	still mineral water or tap water
affettato misto	variety of cold, sliced meats such as salame, cooked ham etc.
affogato al caffè	ice cream with hot espresso coffee
aglio	garlic
agnello	lamb
agnello al forno	roast lamb
albicocche	apricots
ananas	pineapple
anatra	duck
anatra all'arancia	duck à l'orange
anguilla in umido	stewed eel
anguria	water melon
antipasti	starters
antipasti misti	mixed hors d'oeuvres
aperitivo	aperitif
aragosta	lobster
arancia	orange
aranciata	orangeade
aringa	herring
arista di maiale al forno	roast chine of pork
arrosto di tacchino	roast turkey
arrosto di vitello	roast veal
asparagi	asparagus
avocado all'agro	avocado pears with oil and lemon or vinegar
baccalà	dried cod
baccalà alla vicentina	dried cod Vicentine style
bagnacauda	vegetables (esp. raw) in an oil, garlic and anchovy sauce
banana	banana
barbaresco	dry, red wine typical of the Piedmont region

barbera	dark, dry red wine from Piedmont with slightly bitter edge
bardolino	dry, red wine with subtle, aromatic flavour from area near Verona
barolo	dark, dry red wine from Piedmont with slightly bitter edge
basilico	basil
bavarese	ice-cream cake with milk, eggs and fresh cream
bel paese	soft, full-fat white cheese
besciamella	white sauce
bignè	cream puff
birra	beer
birra chiara	light beer e.g. lager
birra grande (½ litro)	large beer (*approx. 1 pint*)
birra piccola (¼ litro)	small beer (*approx. ½ pint*)
birra scura	dark beer e.g. ales, bitter etc.
bistecca	beef steak
bistecca ai ferri	grilled steak
bollito misto	variety of boiled meats with vegetables
braciola di maiale	pork steak
branzino al forno	baked sea bass (*fish*)
brasato	braised beef with herbs
bresaola	dried, salted beef sliced thinly, eaten cold with oil and lemon
brioche	type of croissant
brodo	clear broth
brodo di pollo	chicken broth
brodo vegetale	clear, vegetable broth
budino	pudding
burro	butter
burro di acciughe	anchovy butter
caciotta	tender, white, fat cheese from Central Italy
caffè	coffee
caffè corretto	espresso coffee with a dash of liqueur
caffè lungo	weak espresso coffee
caffè macchiato	espresso coffee with a dash of milk
caffè ristretto	strong espresso coffee
caffellatte	half coffee, half hot milk

calamari in umido	stewed squid
calamaro	squid
calzone	folded pizza with tomato and mozzarella or ricotta inside
camomilla	camomile tea
cannella	cinnamon
cannelloni al forno	rolls of egg pasta stuffed with meat and baked in the oven
cappelle di funghi porcini alla griglia	grilled boletus mushroom caps
cappuccino	espresso coffee with hot foaming milk and cocoa powder
capretto al forno	roast kid
carciofi	artichokes
carciofini sott'olio	little artichokes in oil
carne	meat
carote	carrots
carpaccio	finely sliced beef fillets with oil, lemon and grated parmesan
carré di maiale al forno	roast pork loin
cassata siciliana	Sicilian ice-cream cake with glacé fruit, chocolate and ricotta
castagne	chestnuts
cavoletti di Bruxelles	Brussel sprouts
cavolfiore	cauliflower
cavolo	cabbage
cefalo	mullet
cernia	grouper (*fish*)
champagne	champagne
charlotte	ice-cream cake with milk, eggs, fresh cream, biscuits and fruit
charlotte al cioccolato	chocolate 'charlotte'
charlotte alla frutta	fruit 'charlotte'
chianti	dark red Tuscan wine with a bitterish aftertaste
ciambella	ring-shaped cake
cicoria	chicory
cicorino	small chicory plants
ciliege	cherries
cime di rapa	young leaves of turnip plant
cioccolata	chocolate
cioccolata calda	hot chocolate

cipolle	onions
cocktail di gamberetti	prawn cocktail
conchiglie alla marchigiana	pasta shells in tomato sauce with celery, carrot, parsley and ham
coniglio	rabbit
coniglio arrosto	roast rabbit
coniglio in salmì	rabbit salmi
coniglio in umido	stewed rabbit
consommé	consommé (*concentrated clear broth*)
contorni	vegetables
coperto	cover charge
coppa	cured neck of pork, sliced finely and eaten cold
costata di manzo	beef entrecôte
costata alla fiorentina	Florentine entrecôte
cotechino	spiced pork sausage for boiling
cotoletta (di vitello)	veal cutlet
cotoletta ai ferri	grilled veal cutlet
cotoletta alla milanese	veal cutlet in breadcrumbs
cotoletta alla valdostana	veal cutlet with ham and cheese cooked in breadcrumbs
cotoletta di agnello	lamb cutlet
cotoletta di maiale	pork cutlet
cozze	mussels
cozze alla marinara	mussels in marinade sauce
crema	cream made with eggs and milk
crema al caffè	coffee cream pudding
crema al cioccolato	chocolate cream pudding
crema di funghi	cream of mushroom soup
crema di piselli	cream of pea soup
crema pasticciera	confectioner's custard
creme caramel	crème caramel
crêpe suzette	crêpe suzette
crescente	type of flat, fried Emilian bread made with flour, lard and egg
crespelle	type of savoury pancake filled with white sauce etc.
crespelle ai funghi	savoury pancakes with mushrooms
crespelle al formaggio	savoury pancakes with cheese
crespelle al pomodoro	savoury pancakes with tomato
crostata di frutta	fruit tart

dadi	stock cubes
datteri	dates
degustazione	tasting
degustazione di vini	wine tasting
denominazione di origine controllata	guarantee of quality of wine
dentice al forno	baked dentex (*type of sea bream*)
dessert	dessert
digestivo	digestive liqueur
dolci	cakes, gateaux etc.
endivia belga	Belgian endives
entrecôte (di manzo)	beef entrecôte
fagiano	pheasant
fagioli	beans
fagioli borlotti in umido	fresh borlotti beans cooked in vegetables, herbs and tomato sauce
fagiolini	long, green beans
faraona	guinea fowl
fegato	liver
fegato alla veneta	liver cooked in butter with onions
fegato con salvia e burro	liver cooked in butter and sage
fettuccine	ribbon-shaped pasta
fettuccine al salmone	'fettuccine' with salmon
fettuccine panna e funghi	'fettuccine' with cream and mushrooms
fichi	figs
filetti di pesce persico	fillets of perch
filetti di sogliola	fillets of sole
filetto (di manzo)	fillet of beef
filetto ai ferri	grilled fillet of beef
filetto al cognac	fillet of beef in cognac
filetto al pepe verde	fillet of beef with green pepper
filetto al sangue	rare fillet of beef
filetto ben cotto	well-done fillet of beef
filetto medio	medium fillet of beef
finocchi gratinati	fennel with melted, grated cheese
finocchio	fennel
fonduta	cheese fondue
formaggi misti	variety of cheeses
fragole	strawberries
fragole con gelato *or* **con panna**	strawberries with ice-cream or fresh cream

frappé	whisked fruit or milk drink with crushed ice
frappé al cioccolato	chocolate milk shake
frascati	dry, white wine from area around Rome
frittata	type of omelette
frittata al formaggio	type of cheese omelette
frittata al prosciutto	type of ham omelette
frittata alle erbe	type of herb omelette
frittata alle verdure	type of vegetable omelette
fritto misto	mixed seafood in batter
frittura di pesce	variety of fried fish
frutta	fruit
frutta alla fiamma	fruit flambé
frutta secca	dried nuts and raisins
frutti di bosco	mixture of strawberries, raspberries, mulberries etc.
frutti di mare	seafood
funghi	mushrooms
funghi trifolati	mushrooms fried in garlic and parsley
gamberetti	prawns
gamberi	crayfish
gamberoni	king prawns
gazzosa	clear lemonade
gelatina	gelatine
gelato	ice-cream
gelato con panna	ice-cream with fresh cream
gelato di crema	vanilla-flavoured ice-cream
gelato di frutta	fruit-flavoured ice-cream
gnocchetti verdi (agli spinaci e al gorgonzola)	small flour, potato and spinach dumplings with melted gorgonzola
gnocchi	small flour and potato dumplings
gnocchi al pomodoro	small flour and potato dumplings in tomato sauce
gnocchi alla romana	small milk and semolina dumplings baked with butter
gorgonzola	strong, soft blue cheese from Lombardy
grancevola	spiny spider crab
granchio	crab
granita	drink with crushed ice

granita di caffè	drink with crushed ice and coffee
granita di caffè con panna	drink with crushed ice, coffee and fresh cream
granita di limone	lemon drink with crushed ice
grigliata di pesce	grilled fish
grigliata mista	mixed grill (*meat or fish*)
grissini	thin, crisp stick of bread
gruviera	Gruyère cheese
indivia	endive
insalata	salad
insalata caprese	sliced tomatoes and mozzarella
insalata di funghi porcini	boletus mushroom salad
insalata di mare	seafood salad
insalata di nervetti	boiled beef or veal cut up and served cold with beans and pickles
insalata di pomodori	tomato salad
insalata di riso	rice salad
insalata mista	mixed salad
insalata russa	Russian salad
insalata verde	green salad
involtini	stuffed rolls (*of meat, pastry etc.*)
kiwi	kiwi fruit
lamponi	raspberries
lamponi con gelato *or* **con panna**	raspberries with ice-cream or fresh cream
lasagne al forno	layers of thick, flat pasta baked in tomato, mince and cheese
latte	milk
latte macchiato con cioccolato	hot, foamy milk with a sprinkling of cocoa powder
lattuga	lettuce
leggero	light
legumi	vegetables like beans, peas, lentils etc.
lemonsoda	sparkling lemon drink
lenticchie	lentils
lepre	hare
limonata	lemon-flavoured fizzy drink
limone	lemon
lingua	tongue
lingua salmistrata	tongue in brine rubbed with saltpetre

macedonia di frutta	fruit salad
macedonia di frutta al maraschino	fruit salad in Maraschino
macedonia di frutta con gelato	fruit salad with ice-cream
maiale	pork
maionese	mayonnaise
mandarino	mandarin
mandorla	almond
manzo	beef
marroni	chestnuts
marsala	thick, very sweet wine similar to sherry
marzapane	marzipan
medaglioni di vitello	round pieces of veal
mela	apple
melanzane	aubergines
melanzane alla siciliana	baked aubergine slices with parmesan, tomato sauce and egg
melone	melon
menta	mint
menu	menu
menu turistico	tourist menu
meringata	meringue pie
meringhe con panna	meringues with fresh cream
merlot	very dark red wine with slightly herby flavour, of French origin
merluzzo	cod
merluzzo alla pizzaiola	cod in tomato sauce with anchovies capers and parsley
merluzzo in bianco	boiled cod with oil and lemon
messicani in gelatina	rolls of veal in gelatine
millefoglie	layered pastry slice with confectioner's custard
minestra in brodo	noodle soup
minestrone	thick vegetable and rice (or noodle) broth
mirtilli	bilberries
mirtilli con gelato *or* **con panna**	bilberries with ice-cream or fresh cream
more	mulberries or blackberries
more con gelato *or* **con panna**	mulberries or blackberries with ice-cream or fresh cream

moscato	sweet, sparkling fruity wine
mostarda di Cremona	preserve of glacé fruit in grape must (or sugar) with syrup and mustard
mousse al cioccolato	chocolate mousse
mozzarella	firm, white, milky buffalo cheese in small, round forms
mozzarella in carrozza	slices of bread and mozzarella floured and fried
nasello	hake
nocciole	hazel nuts
noce moscata	nutmeg
noci	walnuts
nodino	veal chop
olio	oil
orata al forno	baked gilthead (*fish*)
origano	oregano
ossobuco	stewed shin of veal
ostriche	oysters
paglia e fieno	mixture of ordinary and green (spinach) 'tagliatelle'
paillard di manzo o vitello	slices of grilled beef or veal
pane	bread
panino	filled roll
parmigiana di melanzane	baked layers of aubergines, tomato sauce, mozzarella and parmesan
parmigiano	parmesan cheese
pasta al forno	pasta baked in white sauce and grated cheese
pasta e fagioli	very thick soup with blended borlotti beans and small pasta rings
pasta e piselli	pasta with peas
pasticcio di fegato d'oca	baked, pasta-covered dish with goose liver
pasticcio di lepre	baked, pasta-covered dish with hare
pasticcio di maccheroni	baked macaroni
pastina in brodo	noodle soup
patate	potatoes
patate arrosto o al forno	roast or baked potatoes
patate fritte	chips
patate in insalata	potato salad
pâté	pâté
pâté di carne	meat pâté

pâté di fegato	liver pâté
pâté di pesce	fish pâté
pecorino	strong, hard ewe's milk cheese
penne	type of pasta similar to macaroni
penne ai quattro formaggi	'penne' with sauce made from 4 cheeses
penne all'arrabbiata	'penne' with tomato and chili pepper sauce
penne panna e prosciutto	'penne' with fresh cream and ham sauce
pepe	pepper (*spice*)
peperoni	pepper (*vegetable*)
peperoni ripieni	stuffed peppers
peperoni sott'olio	peppers in oil
pera	pear
pesca	peach
pesca melba	peach melba
pesce	fish
pesce al cartoccio	fish baked in foil with herbs
pesce in carpione	marinated fish
pinot	light, dry white wine from Veneto region
pinzimonio	variety of whole, raw vegetables eaten with oil and vinegar
piselli	peas
piselli al prosciutto	fresh peas cooked in clear broth, butter, ham and basil
pizza Margherita	pizza with tomato and mozzarella
pizza napoletana	pizza with tomato, mozzarella and anchovies
pizza quattro stagioni	pizza with tomato, mozzarella, ham, mushrooms and artichokes
pizzaiola	slices of cooked beef in tomato sauce, oregano and anchovies
pizzoccheri alla Valtellinese	thin pasta strips with green vegetables, melted butter and cheese
polenta	cornflour boiled in water until firm and cut in slices
polenta e funghi	'polenta' with mushrooms
polenta e latte	'polenta' with milk
polenta e osei	'polenta' with small birds

polenta pasticciata	alternate layers of 'polenta', tomato sauce and cheese
pollo	chicken
pollo alla cacciatora	chicken chasseur
pollo alla diavola	chicken pieces pressed and fried
pollo arrosto *or* **al forno**	roast chicken
polpette	meatballs
polpettone	meat-loaf
pomodori	tomatoes
pomodori ripieni	stuffed tomatoes
pompelmo	grapefruit
porri	leeks
prezzemolo	parsley
primi piatti	first courses
prosciutto cotto	cooked ham
prosciutto crudo *or* **di Parma**	dry-cured ham
prosciutto di Praga	type of dry-cured ham
prosciutto e fichi	dry-cured ham and figs
prosciutto e melone	dry-cured ham and melon
prugne	plums
punte di asparagi all'agro	asparagus tips in oil and lemon
purè di patate	creamed potatoes
quaglie	quails
radicchio	chicory
ragù	sauce made with mince, tomatoes and diced vegetables
rapa	type of white turnip with flavour similar to radish
rapanelli	radishes
ravioli	tiny packets of egg pasta stuffed with meat, cheese etc.
ravioli al pomodoro	'ravioli' in tomato sauce
razza	skate
ricotta	type of cottage cheese
risi e bisi	risotto with peas and little pieces of ham
riso	rice
riso a pomodoro	rice with tomato
riso in brodo	rice in clear broth
risotto	rice cooked in clear broth till broth has completely evaporated

risotto ai funghi	mushroom 'risotto'
risotto al nero di seppia	black risotto (with ink of cuttlefish)
risotto al salmone	salmon 'risotto'
risotto al tartufo	truffle 'risotto'
risotto alla castellana	'risotto' with mushroom, ham, cream and cheese sauce
risotto alla milanese	'risotto' with saffron
roast-beef all'inglese	roast-beef sliced very thinly and served cold with lemon
robiola	type of soft fresh cheese from Lombardy
rognone trifolato	small kidney pieces in garlic, oil and parsley
rosato	rosé wine
rosmarino	rosemary
salame	highly seasoned type of sausage, eaten cold
sale	salt
salmone affumicato	smoked salmon
salsa cocktail	mayonnaise and tomato ketchup sauce for garnishing seafoods
salsa di pomodoro	tomato sauce
salsa tartara	tartar sauce
salsa vellutata	white sauce made with clear broth instead of milk
salsa verde	sauce for meats made with chopped parsley and oil
salsiccia	sausage
salsiccia di cinghiale	wild boar sausage
salsiccia di maiale	pork sausage
saltimbocca alla romana	slices of veal rolled with ham and sage and fried
salvia	sage
sambuca (con la mosca)	liqueur similar to aniseed from Lazio region (with a coffee bean)
sarde ai ferri	grilled sardines
sardine	sardines
scaloppine	veal escalopes
scaloppine ai carciofi	veal escalopes with artichokes
scaloppine ai funghi	veal escalopes with mushrooms
scaloppine al Marsala	veal escalopes in Marsala
scaloppine al prezzemolo	veal escalopes with parsley
scaloppine al vino bianco	veal escalopes in white wine

scamorza alla griglia type of soft cheese, grilled
scampi alla griglia grilled scampi
secco dry
secondi piatti second courses
sedano di Verona Veronese celery
selvaggina game
semifreddo dessert made of ice-cream, sponge etc. and served cold
senape mustard
seppie in umido stewed cuttlefish
servizio compreso service charge included
servizio escluso not including service charge
soave light, dry white wine from region around Lake Garda
sogliola sole
sogliola ai ferri grilled sole
sogliola al burro sole cooked in butter
sogliola alla mugnaia sole cooked in flour and butter
sorbetto sherbet, soft ice-cream
soufflé soufflé
soufflé al formaggio cheese soufflé
soufflé al prosciutto ham soufflé
spaghetti aglio, olio e peperoncino spaghetti with garlic, oil and crushed chili pepper
spaghetti al pesto spaghetti in crushed basil, garlic, oil and parmesan dressing
spaghetti al pomodoro spaghetti in tomato sauce
spaghetti al ragù spaghetti with mince and tomato sauce
spaghetti alla carbonara spaghetti with egg, chopped bacon and cheese sauce
spaghetti alla matriciana spaghetti in minced pork and tomato sauce typical of Rome
spaghetti alla puttanesca spaghetti with anchovies, capers and black olives in tomato sauce
spaghetti alle vongole spaghetti with clams
speck type of dry-cured, smoked ham
spezzatino di vitello veal stew
spiedini small pieces of different meats or fish cooked on the spit
spinaci spinach
spinaci all'agro spinach with oil and lemon

spremuta d'arancia	freshly squeezed orange juice
spremuta di limone	freshly squeezed lemon juice
spumante	sparkling wine like champagne
stracchino	type of soft, fresh cheese from Lombardy
stracciatella	beaten eggs cooked in boiling, clear broth
strudel di mele	apple strudel
succo d'arancia	orange juice
succo di albicocca	apricot juice
succo di pera	pear juice
succo di pesca	peach juice
succo di pompelmo	grapefruit juice
sugo al tonno	tomato sauce with garlic, tuna and parsley
svizzera	hamburger
tacchino ripieno	stuffed turkey
tagliata	finely-cut beef fillet heated in the oven
tagliatelle	thin, flat strips of egg pasta
tagliatelle al basilico	thin, flat strips of egg pasta and chopped basil
tagliatelle al pomodoro	'tagliatelle' with tomato sauce
tagliatelle al ragù	'tagliatelle' with mince and tomato sauce
tagliatelle alla bolognese	'tagliatelle' with mince and tomato sauce
tagliatelle con panna e funghi	'tagliatelle' with cream and ham sauce
tagliatelle rosse	thin, flat strips of egg pasta with chopped red peppers
tagliatelle verdi	thin, flat strips of egg pasta with chopped spinach
tagliolini	thin, soup noodles
tagliolini ai funghi	thin, soup noodles with mushrooms
tagliolini al salmone	thin, soup noodles with salmon
tagliolini alla panna	thin, soup noodles with cream
tartine	little sandwiches
tartufo	round ice-cream covered in cocoa or chocolate
tè	tea
tè con latte	tea with milk

è con limone	tea with lemon
imo	thyme
iramisu	coffee-soaked sponge, egg and Marsala cream and cocoa powder
onno	tuna
orta	tart
orta salata	savoury flan
orta ai carciofi	artichoke flan
orta al cioccolato	chocolate tart
orta al formaggio	cheese flan
orta di mele	apple tart
orta di noci	walnut tart
orta di ricotta	type of cheesecake
orta di zucchine	courgette flan
orta gelato	ice-cream tart
ortellini	small packets of pasta stuffed with pork loin, ham and parmesan
ortellini al pomodoro	'tortellini' with tomato sauce
ortellini al ragù	'tortellini' with mince and tomato sauce
ortellini alla panna	'tortellini' with cream
ortellini in brodo	'tortellini' in clear broth
ortelloni di magro *or* **di ricotta**	packets of pasta stuffed with cheese, parsley, chopped vegetables
ortelloni di zucca	'tortelloni' stuffed with pumpkin
rancio di palombo	smooth hound slice (*fish*)
rancio di pesce spada	swordfish slice
renette col pesto	type of flat spaghetti with crushed basil, garlic, oil, cheese sauce
riglie	mullet
rippa	tripe
rota	trout
rota affumicata	smoked trout
rota al burro	trout cooked in butter
rota alle mandorle	trout with almonds
rota bollita	boiled trout
ıccelletti	small birds wrapped in bacon on cocktail sticks
ıova	eggs
ıova al tegamino con pancetta	fried eggs and bacon
ıova alla coque	boiled eggs
ıova farcite	eggs with tuna, capers and

	mayonnaise filling
uova sode	hard-boiled eggs
uva	grapes
uva bianca	white grapes
uva nera	black grapes
vellutata di asparagi	creamed asparagus with egg yokes
vellutata di piselli	creamed peas with egg yokes
verdura	vegetables
vermicelli	pasta thinner than spaghetti
vino	wine
vino bianco	white wine
vino da dessert	dessert wine
vino da pasto	table wine
vino da tavola	table wine
vino rosé	rosé wine
vino rosso	red wine
vitello tonnato	sliced veal in blended tuna, anchov oil and lemon sauce
vongole	clams
würstel	frankfurter
yogurt	yoghurt
zabaione	cream made from beaten eggs, sug and Marsala
zafferano	saffron
zucca	pumpkin
zucchine	courgettes
zucchine al pomodoro	chopped courgettes in tomato, garli and parsley sauce
zucchine ripiene	stuffed courgettes
zuccotto	ice-cream cake with sponge, fresh cream and chocolate
zuppa	soup
zuppa di cipolle	onion soup
zuppa di cozze	mussel soup
zuppa di lenticchie	lentil soup
zuppa di pesce	fish soup
zuppa di verdura	vegetable soup
zuppa inglese	trifle

SHOPPING

Shops are usually open from 8.30/9am to 1pm and from 3.30/4pm to 7.30/8pm, often later in tourist resorts in the high season. Shop hours may vary slightly according to the region you are in, as will half-day closing, (which is often Monday morning or Thursday afternoon).
There are some differences between Italian and British shops, for example:
Chemists are very expensive (see Health). So if you should need non-medical personal items such as disinfectant, toothpaste, elastoplast, tampons, deodorants etc then it's better to go to a supermarket or to a *drogheria* (drog-eree-a), which is like a chemist and general grocery store combined. If you wish to buy perfumes or sophisticated cosmetic products, you should go to a *profumeria* (pro-foomeree-a). If you want to buy films or get your photos developed go to a photographic shop or to an optician's, NOT to a chemist's.
In Italy you won't find the type of launderette where you can do your own washing and drying. A *tintoria* (teentoree-a) will only accept clothes for dry-cleaning or large items such as bed linen - but not small personal items.
For cigarettes and stamps there is the *tabaccaio* which is simply a specially licensed bar. They close at 8pm (with only a few exceptions) and after this hour cigarettes are almost impossible to find even in big cities.

USEFUL WORDS AND PHRASES

Please refer to the mini-dictionary for individual items you may want to ask for.

audio equipment	il hi-fi	*hy-fy*
baker	il panettiere	*pannet-t-yaireh*
boutique	la boutique	*booteek*
butcher	il macellaio	*machel-la-yo*

bookshop	la libreria	*leebreree-a*
to buy	comprare	*komprarreh*
cake shop	la pasticceria	*pasteecheree-a*
cheap	economico	*ekonomeeko*
chemist *(shop)*	la farmacia	*farmachee-a*
(man)	il farmacista	*farmacheesta*
department store	il grande magazzino	*grandeh magatzeeno*
fashion	la moda	*moda*
fishmonger	il pescivendolo	*peshee-vendolo*
florist	il fioraio	*f-yorra-yo*
grocer	il negoziante di alimentari	*negotzi-anteh dee alleementaree*
ironmonger's	il negozio di ferramenta	*negotzi-o dee fairamenta*
ladies' wear	l'abbigliamento per signora	*lab-beel-yamento pair seen-yora*
menswear	l'abbigliamento da uomo	*lab-beel-yamento da wommo*
newsagent	il giornalaio	*jornala-yo*
pharmacy	il farmacia	*farmachee-a*
receipt	lo scontrino	*skontreeno*
record shop	il negozio di dischi	*negotzi-o dee deeskee*
sale	la svendita, i saldi	*zvendeeta, saldee*
shoe shop	la calzoleria	*kaltzoleree-a*
shop	il negozio	*negotzi-o*
to go shopping	andare a fare la spesa	*andarreh a farreh la spaiza*
special offer	l'offerta speciale	*lof-fairta spechalleh*
to spend	spendere	*spendereh*
stationer	il cartolaio	*kartola-yo*
supermarket	il supermercato	*soopermairkatto*
tailor	il sarto	*sarto*
take-away	da portare via	*da portarreh vee-a*
till	la casa	*kas-sa*
travel agent	l'agenzia di viaggio	*lajentzee-a dee vee-aj-jo*
toyshop	il negozio di giocattoli	*negotzi-o dee jokkat-tollee*

I'd like...
Vorrei...
Vor-ray...

Do you have...?
Ha...?
Ah...?

How much is this?
Quanto costa questo?
Kwannto kosta kwesto?

Do you have any more of these?
Ne ha ancora di questi?
Nay ah ankora dee kwestee?

Have you anything cheaper?
Non ha niente di più economico?
Non ah nyenteh dee pyoo ekonomeeko?

Have you anything larger?
Non ne ha uno più grande?
Non nay ah oono pyoo grandeh?

Have you anything smaller?
Non ne ha uno più piccolo?
Non nay ah oono pyoo peek-kolo?

Does it come in other colours?
C'è anche in altri colori?
Cheh ankeh een ahltree koloree?

Can I try it (them) on?
Posso provarlo (li)?
Pos-so provarloh (lee)?

I'd like to change this please
Vorrei cambiare questo, per favore
Vor-ray kambee-arreh kwesto, pair favvoreh

It's faulty
È difettoso
Eh deefet-tozo

Can I have a refund?
Posso riavere indietro i soldi?
Pos-so ree-avaireh eendee-aytro ee solldee?

REPLIES YOU MAY BE GIVEN

Desidera?
Can I help you?

Mi dispiace quest'articolo è esaurito
I'm sorry, we're out of stock

Questo è tutto quello che abbiamo
This is all we have

La merce venduta non si cambia senza lo scontrino
Goods are not exchanged without a receipt

Diamo solamente buoni acquisto
We only give credit notes

Ha spiccioli?
Do you have any change?

Non ha niente di più piccolo?
Have you anything smaller?

Where is the ... department?
Dov'è il reparto...?
Doveh eel raiparto...?

Could you wrap it for me?
Potrebbe farmi un pacchetto?
Potraib-beh farmee oon pak-ket-to?

Can I have a bag please?
Potrebbe darmi un sacchetto?
Potraib-be darmee oon sak-ket-to?

Where do I pay?
Dove pago?
Doveh paggo?

Can I have a receipt?
Potrebbe darmi lo scontrino?
Potraib-be darmee loh skontreeno?

I'm just looking
Sto solo dando uno sguardo
Stoh solo dando oono zgwarrdo

I'll come back later
Tornerò più tardi
Tornairo pyoo tardee

THINGS YOU'LL SEE OR HEAR

abbigliamento da uomo	men's clothing
abbigliamento per signora	ladies' clothing
agenzia di viaggio	travel agency
alimentari	groceries
bibite	drinks
caffè	coffee
calzature	shoes
cartoleria	stationer's
dolciumi	confectionery, cakes
dozzina	dozen
economico, bon mercato	cheap
elettrodomestici	electrical goods
fai-da-te	Do-it-yourself supplies
fioraio	flower shop
fiori	flowers
forniture per ufficio	office supplies
fresco	fresh
frutta	fruit
giocattoli	toys
grande magazzino	department store
hi-fi	audio equipment
libreria	bookshop
liquori	spirits
macellaio	butcher
macelleria, beccheria	butcher's shop
moda	fashion
moquette	carpets (fitted)
nolo, noleggio	rental
offerta speciale	special offer
panetteria	bakery
pasticceria	cake shop
pellicce	furs

pellicceria	furrier's
pescheria	fish market
piano superiore	upper floor
prezzo	price
prezzo speciale	special price
prima qualità	high quality
qualità	quality
reparto	department
ridotto, ribassato	reduced
riviste	magazines
saldi estivi	summer sales
saldi invernali	winter sales
sartoria	tailor's
snack bar, tavola calda	snack bar
sterlina	pound sterling
svendita	sale
tabacchi	tobacco supplies
tappeti	carpets (rugs)
tè	tea
verdure	vegetables

AT THE HAIRDRESSER'S

Outside an Italian hairdresser's shop there may be one of two signs: either *parrucchiere* or *acconciature.* Hairdressers all have a fixed closing day which varies from town to town. But, unlike shops, they remain open during the lunch hour and close at 7pm. In many hairdressers it is not necessary to make an appointment. To avoid waiting too long, try going during lunch-time or on a rainy day.

USEFUL WORDS AND PHRASES

appointment	l'appuntamento	*lap-poontamento*
beard	la barba	*barba*
blond	biondo	*byohndo*
brush	la spazzola	*spatzola*
comb	il pettine	*pet-teeneh*
conditioner	il balsamo	*bal-sammo*
curlers	i bigodini	*beego-deenee*
curling tongs	l'arricciacapelli	*lareecha-kapel-lee*
curly	riccio	*reecho*
dark	scuro	*skooro*
fringe	la frangia, frangetta	*fran-ja, franjet-ta*
gel	il gel, la gommina	*jel, gom-meena*
hair	i capelli	*kapel-li*
haircut	il taglio (di capelli)	*tal-yo (dee kapel-lee)*
hairdresser	il parrucchiere	*par-rook-kyaireh*
hairdryer	l'asciugacapelli, il phon	*lashooga-kapel-lee, fon*
highlights	i riflessi	*reefles-see*
layered	scalato	*skallatto*
long	lungo	*loongo*
moustache	i baffi	*baf-fee*
parting	la riga	*reega*
perm	la permanente	*pairmanenteh*
shampoo	lo shampoo	*shampoo*

shave	farsi la barba, radersi	*farsee la barba raddersee*
shaving foam	la schiuma da barba	*skyooma da barba*
short	corto	*korto*
styling mousse	la spuma, schiuma	*spooma, skyooma*
toning down of colour	la sfumatura	*sfoomattura*
wavy	ondulato	*ondoolatto*

I'd like to make an appointment
Vorrei prendere un appuntamento
Vor-ray prendereh oon ap-poontamento

Just a trim please
Solo una spuntatina, per favore
Solo oona spoontateena, pair favvoreh

Not too much off
Non tagli troppo
Non tal-yee troppo

A bit more off here please
Un po' più corti qui, per favore
Oon poh pyoo kortee kwee, pair favvoreh

I'd like a cut and blow-dry
Vorrei taglio e messa in piega (con il phon)
Vor-ray tal-yo ay mes-sa een pyaiga (kon eel fon)

I'd like a perm
Vorrei fare la permanente
Vor-ray farreh la pairmanenteh

I'd like highlights
Vorrei fare i riflessi
Vor-ray farreh ee reefles-see

THINGS YOU'LL SEE OR HEAR

asciugare	to dry
asciugare con il phon	to blow-dry
coiffeur	hair stylist
fare uno shampoo colorante	to tint
farsi la barba	to shave
lavare	to wash
messa in piega	set
parrucchiere	hairdresser
parrucchiere per signore	ladies' salon
permanente	perm
salone da parrucchiere	hairdressing salon
salone per uomo, barbiere	men's hairdresser

SPORTS

Whether you enjoy sport as a passive spectator or as an active participant, Italy has a great deal to offer. The Italians are passionate football fans and the championships are played from June to September. Cycling is also a favourite Italian sport and the *Giro d'Italia* – the annual race round the peninsula – takes place during May and June.
Summer sports include fishing, golfing, skin-diving, swimming and tennis. There is no lack of fine beaches in Italy and most of them are well-managed and provide everything for the tourist's enjoyment. There are numerous windsurfing schools where you can take lessons and hire all the necessary equipment, from boards to wetsuits. One of the most notable areas for this sport is Lake Garda.
Italy is a haven for mountain climbers and hill-walkers who will delight in discovering the many beautiful Alpine and Apennine valleys unknown to the average tourist. For winter sports there are excellently equipped skiing resorts in the Dolomites and in the Piedmont and Lombardy regions of Northern Italy.

USEFUL WORDS AND PHRASES

Alps	le Alpi	*alpee*
athletics	l'atletica	*latleteeka*
ball	la palla	*pal-la*
bathing costume	il costume da bagno	*kostoomeh da ban-yo*
beach	la spiaggia	*sp-yaj-ja*
beach umbrella	l'ombrellone	*lombrel-loneh*
bicycle	la bicicletta	*beecheeklet-ta*
binding	l'attacco (degli sci)	*lat-tak-ko (del-yee shee)*
blizzard	la bufera di neve	*boofaira dee naiveh*
canoe	la canoa	*kanno-a*
cross-country-skiing	lo sci di fondo	*shee dee fondo*

deckchair	la sedia a sdraio	*saidee-a a zdra-yo*
diving board	il trampolino	*trampoleeno*
fishing	la pesca	*peska*
fishing rod	la canna da pesca	*kan-na da peska*
flippers	le pinne	*peen-neh*
football	il pallone, calcio	*pal-loneh, kallcho*
football match	la partita di pallone, calcio	*parteeta dee pal-loneh, kallcho*
golf	il golf	*'golf'*
golf course	il campo da golf	*kampo da golf*
gymnastics	la ginnastica	*jeen-nasteeka*
lake	il lago	*laggo*
lift pass	il tesserino per la seggiovia	*tes-sereeno pair la sej-jovee-ah*
mountaineering	l'alpinismo	*lalpeeneezmo*
piste	la pista	*peesta*
racket	la rachetta	*rak-ket-ta*
riding	l'equitazione	*laykweetatzioneh*
rowing boat	la barca a remi	*barka a raimee*
to run	correre	*kor-rereh*
sailboard	il surf	*'surf'*
sailing	la vela	*vaila*
sand	la sabbia	*sab-bee-a*
sea	il mare	*marreh*
to skate	pattinare	*pat-teenarreh*
skating	il pattinaggio	*pat-teenaj-jo*
skating rink	la pista di patti-naggio	*peesta dee pat-teenaj-jo*
to ski	sciare	*shee-arreh*
ski boots	gli scarponi da	*skarponee da shee*
ski lift	la seggiovia	*sej-jovee-a*
skis	gli sci	*shee*
ski-trail	la pista	*peesta*
to skate	pattinare	*pat-teenarreh*
skates	i pattini	*pat-teenee*
sledge	la slitta	*zleeta*
snorkel	il respiratore a tubo	*raispeerattoreh a toobo*

snow	la neve	*naiveh*
to snow	nevicare	*naiveekarreh*
stadium	lo stadio	*staddee-o*
surfboard	il surf	*'surf'*
to swim	nuotare	*nwottarreh*
swimming pool	la piscina	*peesheena*
tennis	il tennis	*ten-nis*
tennis court	il campo da tennis	*kampo da ten-nis*
tennis racket	la racchetta da tennis	*rak-ket-ta da ten-nis*
tent	la tenda	*tenda*
tide	la marea	*marray-a*
volleyball	la pallavolo	*pal-lavolo*
walking	camminare	*kam-meenarreh*
water skis	gli sci d'acqua	*shee dakkwa*
water skiing	lo sci acquatico	*shee akkwateeko*
wave	l'onda	*lohnda*
windsurfing	il windsurf	*'windsurf'*
winter sports	gli sport invernali	*sport eenvairnallee*
yacht	lo yacht	*'yacht'*

How do I get to the beach?
Potrebbe indicarmi la strada per la spiaggia?
Potraib-beh eendeekarmee la strad-da pair la sp-yaj-ja

How deep is the water here?
Quant'è profonda qui l'acqua?
Kwannteh profonda kwee lakkwa?

Is there an indoor/outdoor pool here?
C'è una piscina coperta/scoperta?
Cheh oona peesheena kopairta/skopairta?

Is it dangerous to swim here?
È pericoloso nuotare qui?
Eh paireekolozo nwottarreh kwee?

Can I fish here?
Posso pescare qui?
Pos-so peskarreh kwee?

Do I need a licence?
C'è bisogno della licenza di pesca?
Cheh beezon-yo del-la leechentza dee peska?

I would like to hire a bike
Vorrei noleggiare una bicicletta
Vor-ray nolej-jarreh oona beecheeklet-ta

How much does it cost per hour/day?
Quanto costa all'ora/al giorno?
Kwannto kosta al ora/al jorno?

When does the lift start?
À che ora si aprono gli impianti?
Ah kay ora see approno l-yee eempee-antee?

How much is a daily/weekly lift pass?
Quanto costa un giornaliero/un settimanale?
Kwannto kosta oon jornal-yairo/oon set-tee-manalleh?

I would like to take skiing lessons
Vorrei prendere lezioni di sci
Vor-ray prendereh letzionee dee shee

Where are the nursery slopes?
Dove sono le discese per principianti?
Doveh sono lay deeshaizeh pair preencheepee-antee?

Is it very steep?
È molto ripido?
Eh molto reepeedo?

Where can I hire...?
Dove posso prendere in affitto...?
Doveh pos-so prendereh een af-feet-to...?

THINGS YOU'LL SEE OR HEAR

alla seggiovia	to the ski lift
andare in barca a vela	to sail
alta marea	high tide
bassa marea	low tide
bufera di neve	blizzard
ciclista	cyclist
correnti pericolose	dangerous currents
cumulo di neve	snowdrift
disgelo	thaw
divieto di balneazione	no bathing
divieto di pesca	no fishing
nevicata	snowfall
noleggio di barche	boat hire
noleggio di biciclette	cycle hire
pedoni	pedestrians
pericolo	danger
pericolo di valanghe	danger of avalanches
piscina	swimming pool
piscina coperta	indoor swimming pool
piscina scoperta	open air swimming pool
pista ciclabile	cycle path
pista per slitte	toboggan run
praticare il windsurf	to windsurf
pronto soccorso	first aid
remare	to row
sci di fondo	cross-country skiing
trampolino	diving board, ski jump
tuffarsi	to dive
vietato bagnarsi	no bathing

POST OFFICE

Post offices are open from 8.15am until 2pm, central branches stayir open until 4pm. Letter boxes in Italy are yellow. Stamps can be boug at the post office or, more conveniently, at any tobacconist (*tabaccai* These are easily identifiable by the sign displayed outside – a whi 'T' on a black background. Remember that a postcard with a lot writing on it requires a more expensive stamp than one which simp says 'wish you were here' etc.

USEFUL WORDS AND PHRASES

airmail	la posta aerea	*posta ah-airay-a*
collection	la levata	*levatta*
counter	lo sportello	*sportel-lo*
customs form	il modulo per la dogana	*modoolo pair la doganna*
delivery	la consegna	*konsenya*
deposit	il deposito	*daipozeeto*
express letter	l'espresso	*lespres-so*
form	il modulo	*modoolo*
insured letter	l'assicurata	*las-seekooratta*
letter	la lettera	*let-tera*
letter box	la cassetta delle lettere	*cas-set-tah del-leh let-tereh*
mail	la posta, corrispondenza	*posta, korreespondentza*
main post office	l'ufficio postale centrale	*loof-feecho postalleh chentralleh*
money order	il vaglia postale	*val-ya postalleh*
package	il pacchetto	*pak-ket-to*
parcel	il pacco	*pak-ko*
post, mail	la posta	*posta*
postage rates	le tariffe postali	*tareef-feh postallee*

postal order	il vaglia postale	*val-ya postalleh*
postcard	la cartolina	*kartoleena*
postcode	il codice postale	*kodeecheh postalleh*
poste-restante	fermo posta	*fairmo posta*
postman	il postino	*posteeno*
post office	l'ufficio postale	*loof-feecho postalleh*
registered letter	la raccomandata	*rak-komandatta*
savings	i risparmi	*reesparmee*
stamp	il francobollo	*frankobol-lo*
surface mail	la posta ordinaria	*posta ordeenaree-a*
telegram	il telegramma	*telegram-ma*
telephone	il telefono	*telefono*
telephone kiosk	la cabina telefonica	*kabeena telefoneeka*
withdrawal	il prelievo	*prail-yaivo*

How much is a letter/postcard to...?
Quanto costa spedire una lettera/una cartolina a...?
Kwannto kosta spedeereh oona let-tera/oona kartoleena a...?

I would like three 600 lira stamps
Vorrei tre francobolli da 600 lire
Vor-ray treh frankobol-lee da 600 leereh

I want to register this letter
Vorrei spedire una raccomandata/un'assicurata
Vor-ray spedeereh oona rak-komandatta/oon as-seekooratta

I want to send this parcel to...
Vorrei spedire questo pacco a...
Vor-ray spedeereh kwesto pak-ko a...

How long does the mail to ... take?
Quanto tempo impiega una lettera per...?
Kwannto tempo eempyaiga oona let-tera pair...?

Where can I mail this?
Dove posso imbucare questo?
Doveh pos-so eembookarreh kwesto?

I want to make an international call
Vorrei fare una telefonata internazionale
Vor-ray farreh oona telefonatta eentairnatzionalleh

Is there any mail for me?
C'è posta per me?
Cheh posta pair meh?

I'd like to send a telegram
Vorrei spedire una telegramma
Vor-ray spedeereh oona telegram-ma

This is to go airmail
Deve essere spedito per via aerea
Daiveh es-saireh spedeeto pair vee-a ah-airay-a

THINGS YOU'LL SEE OR HEAR

affrancatura	postage
affrancatura per l'estero	postage abroad
cabina telefonica	telephone box
cartolina	postcard
codice (di avviamento) postale	postal code
deposito	deposit
destinatario	addressee
fermo posta	poste restante
francobollo	stamp
indirizzo	address
lettera	letter
orario di apertura	opening hours
mittente	sender
pacchetto	package
posta aerea	airmail
postagiro	postal transfer, giro
posta assicurata	insured mail
posta	mail
riempire/compilare	to fill in
sportello pacchi	parcels counter
tariffa	rate, charge
tariffa interna	inland postage
telefono	telephone
telegrammi	telegrams

TELEPHONE

In some Italian telephone boxes you can phone with L.100 and L.200 lire pieces whereas others will require *gettoni* - tokens each worth L.200. You can also use these as normal currency, so don't be alarmed if you receive one in your change when shopping. When you need *gettoni* you can ask for them in any bar. If you need to make a long-distance phone-call it is better to go to an office of the national Italian telephone company, the SIP, or ask in a bar if the barman has a telephone 'a scatti'. To telephone the UK, dial 0044 followed by the area code (but exclude the 0 which prefixes all UK area codes) and the number you want. To call a USA number, dial 1 followed by the area code and the subscriber's number.

The tones you'll hear when telephoning Italy are:
Dialling tone: two very short tones at regular intervals;
Ringing tone: one single, short tone at regular intervals;
Engaged: short rapid pips;
Unobtainable: short rapid pips (but different from the engaged tone).

USEFUL WORDS AND PHRASES

call	la telefonata	*telefonatta*
to call	telefonare	*telefonarreh*
code	il prefisso	*praifees-so*
crossed line	l'interferenza	*leentairfairentza*
to dial	fare/formare il numero	*farreh/formarreh eel noomero*
dialling tone	il segnale di libero	*sen-yalleh dee leebairo*
engaged tone	il segnale di occupato	*sen-yalleh dee ok-koopatto*
emergency	l'emergenza	*lemairjentza*
enquiries	il servizio informazioni telefoniche	*sairveetzi-o eenformatzioneh telefoneekeh*
extension	l'interno	*leentairno*

ternational call	la chiamata internazionale	*kyamatta eentairnatzionalleh*
perator	il centralino	*chentraleeno*
ceiver	il ricevitore	*reechaiveetoreh*
verse charge call	la chiamata a carico del destinatario	*kyamatta ah karreeko del desteenattaree-o*
nging tone	il segnale di libero	*sen-yalleh dee leebairo*
lephone	il telefono	*telefono*
lephone box	la cabina telefonica	*kabeena telefoneeka*
lephone directory	la guida telefonica	*gweeda telefoneeka*
rong number	il numero sbagliato	*noomero zbal-yatto*

here is the nearest phone box?
ov'è la cabina telefonica più vicina?
veh la kabeena telefoneeka pyoo veecheena?

there a telephone directory?
'è una guida telefonica?
heh oona gweeda telefoneeka?

would like the directory for...
rrei l'elenco telefonico di...
r-ray lelenko telefoneeko dee...

an I call abroad from here?
sso fare una telefonata internazionale da qua?
s-so farreh oon telefonatta eentairnatzionalleh da kwah?

ow much is a call to...?
uanto costa telefonare a...?
wannto kosta telefonarreh ah...?

would like to reverse the charges
ı metta a carico del destinatario
a met-ta ah karreeko del desteenattaree-o

I would like a number in...
Ho bisogno del numero di un abbonato di...
Oh beezon-yo del noomero dee oon ab-bonatto dee...

Hello, this is ... speaking
Pronto, sono...
Pronto, sono...

Is that...?
Chi parla? È...?
Kee parla? Eh...?

Speaking
Sono io
Sono ee-o

I would like to speak to...
Vorre parlare con...
Vor-ray parlarreh kon...

Extension ... please
Interno ..., per favore
Eentairno ..., pair favvoreh

Please tell him ... called
Per cortesia, gli dica che ha telefonato...
Pair kortaizee-a lyee deeka kay ah telefonatto...

Ask him to call me back please
Gli dica di ritelefonarmi, per favore
Lyee deeka dee reetelefonarmee, pair favvoreh

My number is...
Il mio numero è...
Eel mee-o noomero eh...

Do you know where he is?
Non sa dov'è?
Non sah doveh?

When will he be back?
Quando tornerà?
Kwanndo tornaira?

Could you leave him a message?
Potrebbe lasciargli un messaggio?
Potraib-beh lasharlyee oon mes-saj-jo?

I'll ring back later
Ritelefonerò più tardi
Reetelefonairo pyoo tardee

Sorry, wrong number
Mi scusi, ho sbagliato numero
Mee skoosee, oh zbal-yatto noomero

The phone is out of order
Il telefono è fuori servizio
Eel telefono eh fworee sairveetzi-o

Please connect me to...
Mi passa ... per favore
Mee pas-sa ... pair favvoreh

REPLIES YOU MAY BE GIVEN

Sono io
Speaking

Con chi vuole parlare?
Who do you want to speak to?

Chi parla?
Who's calling?

Attenda in linea, prego
Hold the line, please

Mi dispiace, non c'è
I'm sorry, he's not in

Tornerà alle...
He'll be back at...

Posso richiamarla?
Can I call you back?

Ha sbagliato numero
You've got the wrong number

THINGS YOU'LL SEE OR HEAR

all'estero	abroad
cabina telefonica	telephone box
centralino	local exchange, operator
chiamata	call
chiamata d'emergenza	emergency call
chiamata in teleselezione	direct dialling
chiamata interurbana	long-distance call
disco (combinatore)	dial
fare il numero	to dial
fuori servizio	out of order
gancio	hook
gettoni	telephone tokens
guida telefonica	telephone directory
incendio	fire
inserire	to insert
locale	local
moneta	coins
numero	number
occupato	engaged
Pagine Gialle	Yellow Pages
pompieri	fire brigade
prefisso	code
ricevitore	receiver
segnale di libero	ringing tone
servizio guasti	faults service
sia breve!	be brief!
sollevare (il ricevitore)	to lift (the receiver)
tariffa	charges
telefono	telephone
telefono all'estero	telephone abroad
telefonata urbana	local call
unità	unit

HEALTH

Under the EEC Social Security regulations visitors from the UK are entitled to medical treatment on the same basis as Italians themselves. Apply to the DHSS for a CM1 at least 6 months befor travelling. The DHSS will then supply you with an E111, whicl you take with you to Italy. In Italy you can get information from th local Health Unit, the USL (Unità Sanitaria Locale).
If you should need medical or dental treatment, hand your E111 t the USL and you will be given a certificate of entitlement. Ask t see a list of the scheme's doctors and dentists. You will be entitle to treatment from any of these, free of charge. For prescribed medicine a standard charge will be made at the chemist's. If you do not ge the certificate from the local Health Office, you will have to pay fc treatment and getting refunds later can be much more problemati In any case the refund would only be partial. See also the paragrap on chemists in the Shopping Section. If a doctor thinks you nee hospital treatment, he will give you a certificate *(proposta di ricovero)* This entitles you to free treatment in certain hospitals, a list of whic will be available at the USL. If you cannot contact the USL offic before going into hospital, show the E111 to the hospital authoriti and ask them to get in touch with the USL about your right to fre treatment.

USEFUL WORDS AND PHRASES

accident	l'incidente	*leencheedenteh*
ambulance	l'ambulanza	*lamboolantza*
anaemic	anemico	*annemeeko*
appendicitis	l'appendicite	*lap-pendeecheeteh*
appendix	l'appendice	*lap-pendeecheh*
aspirin	l'aspririna	*laspeereena*
asthma	l'asma	*lahzma*
backache	il mal di schiena	*mal dee skyaina*
bandage	la fascia, benda	*fasha, benda*

bite ***(of insect)***	la punctura	*poontura*
(of dog, snake)	la morsicatura	*morseekattura*
bladder	la vescica	*vesheeka*
blister	la vescica	*vesheeka*
blood	il sangue	*sangway*
blood donor	il donatore di sangue	*donatoreh dee sangway*
burn	la bruciatura	*broo-chattura*
cancer	il cancro	*kankro*
chemist ***(shop)***	la farmacia	*farmachee-a*
(man)	il farmacista	*farmacheesta*
chest	il petto	*pet-to*
chickenpox	la varicella	*varreechel-la*
cold	il raffreddore	*raf-fred-doreh*
concussion	la commozione cerebrale	*kom-motzioneh chairebralleh*
constipation	la stitichezza	*steeteeketza*
contact lenses	le lenti a contatto	*lentee ah kontat-to*
corn	il callo	*kal-lo*
cough	la tosse	*tohs-seh*
cut	il taglio	*tal-yo*
dentist	il dentista	*denteesta*
diabetes	il diabete	*dee-abetteh*
diarrhoea	la diarrea	*dee-array-a*
doctor	il dottore, medico	*dot-toreh, medeeko*
earache	il mal d'orecchio	*mal dorrek-kyo*
fever	la febbre	*faib-breh*
filling	la piombatura	*pyombattura*
first aid	la cassetta di pronto soccorso	*kas-set-ta dee pronto sok-korso*
flu	l'influenza	*leenfloo-entza*
fracture	la frattura	*frat-tura*
German measles	la rosolia	*rozolee-a*
glasses	gli occhiali	*okk-yallee*
haemorrhage	l'emorragia	*laimor-rajee-a*
hayfever	il raffreddore da fieno	*raf-fred-doreh dah fyaino*
headache	il mal di testa	*mal dee testa*

heart	il cuore	*kworreh*
heart attack	l'infarto	*leenfarto*
hospital	l'ospedale	*lospedalleh*
ill	malato	*malatto*
indigestion	la cattiva digestione	*katteeva deejesti-oneh*
injection	l'iniezione	*leen-yetzioneh*
itch	il prurito	*prooreeto*
kidney	il rene	*raineh*
lung	il polmone	*polmoneh*
lump	il nodulo	*nodoolo*
measles	il morbillo	*morbeel-lo*
migraine	l'emicrania	*laimeekranee-a*
mumps	gli orecchioni	*orrek-kyohnee*
nausea	la nausea	*now-zay-a*
nurse	l'infermiera	*leenfairmee-aira*
operation	l'operazione	*lopairatzioneh*
optician	l'ottico	*lot-teeko*
pain	il dolore	*doloreh*
penicillin	la penicillina	*peneecheel-leena*
plaster	il gesso	*jes-so*
pneumonia	la polmonite	*polmoneeteh*
pregnant	incinta	*eencheenta*
prescription	la ricetta	*reechet-ta*
rheumatism	il reumatismo	*ray-oomateezmo*
scald	la scottatura	*skot-tatura*
scratch	il graffio	*graf-fee-o*
smallpox	il vaiolo	*vy-ollo*
sore throat	il mal di gola	*mal dee gohla*
splinter	la scheggia	*skej-ja*
sprain	la slogatura	*zloggatura*
	lo strappo muscolare	*strap-po mooskolarreh*
sting	la puntura	*poontura*
stomach	lo stomaco	*stomakko*
temperature	la febbre	*faib-breh*
tonsils	le tonsille	*tonseel-leh*
toothache	il mal di denti	*mal dee dentee*
travel sickness	il mal d'auto	*mal douto*

ulcer	l'ulcera	*loolchaira*
vaccination	la vaccinazione	*vacheenatzioneh*
to vomit	vomitare	*vomeetarreh*
whooping cough	la pertosse	*pairtohs-seh*

I have a pain in...
Mi fa male...
Mee fah malleh...

I do not feel well
Non mi sento bene
Non mee sento beneh

I feel faint
Mi sento svenire
Mee sento zveneereh

I feel sick
Ho la nausea
Oh la now-zay-a

I feel dizzy
Mi gira la testa
Mee jeera la testa

It hurts here
Mi fa male qui
Mee fah malleh kwee

It's a sharp pain
È un dolore acuto
Eh oon doloreh akooto

It hurts all the time
Mi fa continuamente male
Mee fah konteenoo-amenteh malleh

It only hurts now and then
Non mi fa sempre male
Non mee fah sempreh malleh

It hurts when you touch it
Mi fa male quando lo tocca
Mee fah malleh kwanndo loh tohk-ka

It hurts more at night
Mi fa male di più di notte
Mee fah malleh dee pyoo dee not-teh

It stings
Brucia
Broocha

It aches
Fa male
Fah malleh

I need a prescription for...
Ho bisogno della ricetta per...
Oh beezon-yo del-la reechet-ta pair...

I normally take...
Generalmente prendo...
Jenairalmenteh prendo...

I'm allergic to...
Sono allergico a...
Sono al-lairjeekoh ah...

Have you got anything for...?
Ha qualcosa per...?
Ah kwallkoza pair...?

)o I need a prescription for...?
;'è bisogno della ricetta per...?
;heh beezon-yo del-la reechet-ta pair...?

REPLIES YOU MAY BE GIVEN

Please write down when and how I must take the medicine
Per piacere mi scriva quando e come devo prendere la medicina

...compresse alla volta
...tablets at a time

Da inghiottire/da masticare
With water/chew them

Una/due/tre volte al giorno
Once/twice/three times a day

Prima di andare a letto
At bedtime

Al mattino
In the morning

Cosa prende normalmente?
What do you normally take?

Per questo c'è bisogno della ricetta
You need a prescription for that

Non può trovarlo qui
You can't get that here

Penso che lei debba andare dal medico
I think you should see the doctor

THINGS YOU'LL SEE OR HEAR

ambulanza	ambulance
anticamera	waiting room
autoambulanza	ambulance
caso d'emergenza	emergency case
clinica	clinic
dentista	dentist
ginecologo	gynaecologist
orario di visite	visiting hours
ospedale	hospital
otorinolaringoiatra	ear, nose and throat specialist
ottico	optician
pronto soccorso	first aid, casualty ward
specialista	specialist

CONVERSION TABLES

DISTANCES

Distances are marked in kilometres. To convert kilometres to miles, divide the km. by 8 and multiply by 5 (one km. being five-eighths of a mile). Convert miles to km. by dividing the miles by 5 and multiplying by 8. A mile is 1609m. (1.609km.).

km.	miles *or* km.	miles
1.61	**1**	0.62
3.22	**2**	1.24
4.83	**3**	1.86
6.44	**4**	2.48
8.05	**5**	3.11
9.66	**6**	3.73
11.27	**7**	4.35
12.88	**8**	4.97
14.49	**9**	5.59
16.10	**10**	6.21
32.20	**20**	12.43
48.28	**30**	18.64
64.37	**40**	24.85
80.47	**50**	31.07
160.93	**100**	62.14
321.90	**200**	124.30
804.70	**500**	310.70
1609.34	**1000**	621.37

Other units of length:

1 centimetre	= 0.39 in.	1 inch	= 25.4 millimetres
1 metre	= 39.37 in.	1 foot	= 0.30 metre (30 cm.)
10 metres	= 32.81 ft.	1 yard	= 0.91 metre

WEIGHTS

The unit you will come into most contact with is the kilogram (kilo), equivalent to 2 lb 3 oz. To convert kg. to lbs., multiply by 2 and add one-tenth of the result (thus, 6 kg x 2 = 12 + 1.2, or 13.2 lbs). One ounce is about 28 grams, and 1 lb is 454 g. One UK hundredweight is almost 51 kg; one USA cwt is 45 kg. One UK ton is 1016 kg (USA ton = 907 kg).

grams	ounces
50	1.76
100	3.53
250	8.81
500	17.63

ounces	grams
1	28.3
2	56.7
4	113.4
8	226.8

kg.	lbs. *or* kg.	lbs.
0.45	**1**	2.20
0.91	**2**	4.41
1.36	**3**	6.61
1.81	**4**	8.82
2.27	**5**	11.02
2.72	**6**	13.23
3.17	**7**	15.43
3.63	**8**	17.64
4.08	**9**	19.84
4.53	**10**	22.04
9.07	**20**	44.09
11.34	**25**	55.11
22.68	**50**	110.23
45.36	**100**	220.46

LIQUIDS

Motorists from the UK will be used to seeing petrol priced per litr (and may even know that one litre is about $1\frac{3}{4}$ pints). One 'imperia gallon is roughly $4\frac{1}{2}$ litres, but USA drivers must remember that th American gallon is only 3.8 litres (1 litre = 1.06 US quart). In th following table, imperial gallons are used:

litres	gals. *or* l.	gals.
4.54	**1**	0.22
9.10	**2**	0.44
13.64	**3**	0.66
18.18	**4**	0.88
22.73	**5**	1.10
27.27	**6**	1.32
31.82	**7**	1.54
36.37	**8**	1.76
40.91	**9**	1.98
45.46	**10**	2.20
90.92	**20**	4.40
136.38	**30**	6.60
181.84	**40**	8.80
227.30	**50**	11.00

TYRE PRESSURES

lb/sq.in.	15	18	20	22	24
kg/sq.cm.	1.1	1.3	1.4	1.5	1.7

lb/sq.in.	26	28	30	33	35
kg/sq.cm.	1.8	2.0	2.1	2.3	2.5

AREA

The average tourist isn't all that likely to need metric area conversions, but with more 'holiday home' plots being bought overseas nowadays it might be useful to know that 1 square metre = 10.8 square feet, and that the main unit of land area measurement is a hectare (which is 2½ acres). The hectare is 10,000 sq.m. - for convenience, visualise something roughly 100 metres or yards square. To convert hectares to acres, divide by 2 and multiply by 5 (and vice-versa).

hectares	acres *or* ha.	acres
0.4	**1**	2.5
2.0	**5**	12.4
4.1	**10**	24.7
20.2	**50**	123.6
40.5	**100**	247.1

TEMPERATURE

To convert centigrade or Celsius degrees into Fahrenheit, the accurate method is to multiply the °C figure by 1.8 and add 32. Similarly, to convert °F to °C, subtract 32 from the °F figure and divide by 1.8. This will give you a truly accurate conversion, but takes a little time in mental arithmetic! See the table below. If all you want is some idea of how hot it is forecast to be in the sun, simply double the °C figure and add 30; the °F result will be overstated by a degree or two when the answer is in the 60-80°F range, while 90°F should be 86°F.

°C	°F	°C	°F	
-10	14	25	77	
0	32	30	86	
5	41	36.9	98.4	body temperature
10	50	40	104	
20	68	100	212	boiling point

CLOTHING SIZES

Slight variations in sizes, let alone European equivalents of UK/USA sizes, will be found everywhere so be sure to check before you buy. The following tables are approximate:

Women's dresses and suits

UK	10	12	14	16	18	20
Europe	**36**	**38**	**40**	**42**	**44**	**46**
USA	8	10	12	14	16	18

Men's suits and coats

UK/USA	36	38	40	42	44	46
Europe	**46**	**48**	**50**	**52**	**54**	**56**

Women's shoes

UK	4	5	6	7	8
Europe	**37**	**38**	**39**	**41**	**42**
USA	5½	6½	7½	8½	9½

Men's shoes

UK/USA	7	8	9	10	11
Europe	**41**	**42**	**43**	**44**	**45**

Men's shirts

UK/USA	14	14½	15	15½	16	16½	17
Europe	**36**	**37**	**38**	**39**	**41**	**42**	**43**

Women's sweaters

UK/USA	32	34	36	38	40
Europe	**36**	**38**	**40**	**42**	**44**

Waist and chest measurements

Inches	28	30	32	34	36	38	40	42	44	4
Cms	71	76	80	87	91	97	102	107	112	11

MINI–DICTIONARY

accelerator l'acceleratore
accident l'incidente
accommodation l'alloggio, il posto
ache il dolore
adaptor *(electrical)* il riduttore
address l'indirizzo
adhesive l'adesivo
Adriatic adriatico
after dopo
after-shave il dopobarba
again di nuovo
air l'aria
air freshener il deodorante
air hostess l'hostess
air-conditioning l'aria condizionata
aircraft l'aereo
airline la linea aerea
airport l'aeroporto
alcohol l'alcool
all tutto
almost quasi
alone solo, da solo
already già
always sempre
am: I am sono
ambulance l'ambulanza
America l'America
American americano
and e
ankle la caviglia
anorak la giacca a vento
another un altro, un'altra
anti-freeze l'antigelo
antique shop il negozio di antiquariato
antiseptic l'antisettico
aperitif l'aperitivo
appendicitis l'appendicite
appetite l'appetito
apple la mela
application form il modulo di domanda
appointment l'appuntamento
apricot l'albicocca
are: we are siamo
  they are sono
  you are *(singular familiar)* sei
  (singular polite) Leì è
  (plural familiar) siete
  (plural polite) Loro sono
arm il braccio
art l'arte
art gallery la galleria d'arte
artist l'artista
ashtray il portacenere
asleep addormentato
  he's asleep dorme
aspirin l'aspirina
at: at the station alla stazione
  at 3 o'clock alle tre
  at night di notte
attractive attraente
aunt la zia
Australia l'Australia
Austria l'Austria
Austrian austriaco
automatic automatico
away: is it far away? è lontano?
  go away! vattene!
awful terribile, orribile
axe l'ascia
axle il semiasse

baby il bambino, il bimbo
back *(not front)* la parte

posteriore
(body) la schiena
bacon la pancetta
bacon and eggs uova con pancetta
bad cattivo
bait l'esca
bake cuocere (al forno)
baker il panettiere
balcony il balcone
ball *(for playing)* la palla
(dance) il ballo
ball-point pen la penna a sfera
banana la banana
band *(musicians)* la banda
bandage la fascia, la benda
bank la banca
banknote la banconota
bar la sbarra
bar of chocolate la tavoletta di cioccolata
barbecue il barbecue
(occasion) una grigliata all'aperto
barber il barbiere
bargain un affare
(cheap thing) l'occasione
basement il seminterrato
basin il lavabo, il lavandino
basket il cestino
(supermarket) il cestello
bath il bagno
to have a bath fare il bagno
bath salts i sali da bagno
bathing hat la cuffia da bagno
bathroom il bagno
battery la batteria
beach la spiaggia
beans i fagioli
beard la barba
because perché
bed il letto
bed linen la biancheria da letto
bedroom la camera da letto
beef il manzo
beer la birra
before prima
beginner il principiante
behind dietro
beige beige
bell *(church)* la campana
(door) il campanello
Belgian belga
Belgium il Belgio
belt la cintura
(technical) la cinghia
beside accanto a, vicino a
better: migliore
between fra
bicycle la bicicletta
big grande
bikini il bikini
bill il conto
bin liner il sacchetto per la pattumiera
bindings *(ski)* gli attacchi
bird l'uccello
birthday il compleanno
happy birthday! buon compleanno!
birthday card il cartoncino di buon compleanno
biscuit il biscotto
bite *(verb)* mordere
(insect) pungere
(noun) il morso
(of an insect) la puntura
bitter amaro
black nero
blackberry la mora
blackcurrant il ribes nero
blanket la coperta
bleach *(verb)* candeggiare
(noun) la candeggina
blind *(cannot see)* cieco

(window) la tenda avvolgibile
blister la vescica
blood il sangue
blouse la camicetta
blue azzurro
(darker) blu
boat la nave
(smaller) la barca
body il corpo
(corpse) il cadavere
boil bollire
bolt *(verb)* chiudere con il catenaccio
(noun: on door) il catenaccio
bone l'osso
(fish) la spina
bonnet *(car)* il cofano
book *(noun)* il libro
(verb) prenotare
booking office *(railway station)* la biglietteria
(theatre etc) il botteghino
bookshop la libreria
boot *(car)* il portabagagli
(footwear) lo stivale
border il confine
boring noioso
born: I was born in... sono nato a...
both: both of them tutti e due
both...and... sia...che...
bottle la bottiglia
bottle-opener l'apribottiglia
bottom il fondo
bowl la scodella
(mixing bowl) la terrina
box la scatola
(of wood etc) la cassetta
boy il ragazzo
boyfriend il ragazzo
bra il reggiseno
bracelet il braccialetto
braces le bretelle
brake *(noun)* il freno
(verb) frenare
brandy il brandy
bread il pane
breakdown *(car)* il guasto
(nervous) l'esaurimento nervoso
breakfast la colazione
breathe respirare
I can't breathe non posso respirare
bridge il ponte
briefcase la cartella
brochure l'opuscolo
broken rotto
brooch la spilla
brother il fratello
brown marrone
bruise il livido
brush *(noun)* la spazzola
(verb) spazzolare
bucket il secchio
building l'edificio
bumper il paraurti
burn *(verb)* bruciare
(skin) bruciare, scottare
(noun) la bruciatura
(on skin) la scottatura
bus l'autobus
bus station la stazione delle autolinee
business l'affare
it's none of your business non sono affari tuoi
busker il suonatore ambulante
busy *(occupied)* occupato
(active: of person) occupato
(of street) animato
but ma
butcher il macellaio
butter il burro
button il bottone

buy comprare
by: by the door vicino alla porta
by myself da solo
by Friday entro venerdì

cabbage il cavolo
cable car la funivia
(on rail) la funicolare
cafe il caffè, il bar
cagoule il K-way ®
cake la torta
cake shop la pasticceria
calculator il calcolatore
camera la macchina fotografica
campsite il campeggio
camshaft l'albero a camme
can *(able)* potere
(tin) la lattina
can I have...? posso avere...?
Canada il Canada
Canadian canadese
canal il canale
cancer il cancro
candle la candela
canoe la canoa
cap il berretto
car l'auto, la macchina
caravan la roulotte
carburettor il carburatore
card il biglietto
cardigan il cardigan
careful attento
be careful! stia attento!
carpet il tappeto
carriage *(train)* la carrozza, il vagone
carrot la carota
carry-cot il porte-enfant
case la valigia
cash contanti
(change) gli spiccioli
to pay cash pagare in contanti
cassette la cassetta
cassette player il mangianastri
castle il castello
cat il gatto
cathedral la cattedrale
cauliflower il cavolfiore
cave la grotta
cemetery il cimitero
certificate il certificato
chair la sedia
chambermaid la cameriera
chamber music la musica da camera
change *(money)* cambiare
(clothes) cambiarsi
Channel il canale della Manica
cheap economico, a buon mercato
cheers! alla salute!, cin cin!
cheese il formaggio
chemist *(shop)* la farmacia
cheque l'assegno
cheque book il libretto degli assegni
cheque card la carta assegni
cherry la ciliegia
chess gli scacchi
chest il petto
chewing gum la gomma americana, il chewing-gum
chicken il pollo
child il bambino
china la porcellana
(crockery) le porcellane
China la Cina
Chinese cinese
chips le patatine fritte
chocolate la cioccolata
box of chocolates la scatola di cioccolatini

bar of chocolate la tavoletta di cioccolata
chop *(food)* la costoletta
(to cut) tagliare (a pezzetti)
church la chiesa
cigar il sigaro
cigarette la sigaretta
cinema il cinema
city la città
city centre il centro della città
class la classe
classical music la musica classica
clean pulito
clear chiaro
(clean) sgombro
is that clear? è chiaro?
clever bravo
clock l'orologio
close *(near)* vicino
(stuffy) soffocante
close *(verb)* chiudere
the shop is closed il negozio è chiuso
clothes i vestiti
club *(society)* il circolo, il club
(golf etc) il circolo
(cards) fiori
clutch la frizione
coach la corriera
(of train) la carrozza
coach station la stazione delle corriere
coat il capotto
coathanger la stampella
cockroach lo scarafaggio
coffee il caffè
coin la moneta
cold *(illness)* il raffreddore
(adj) freddo
collar il colletto
collection *(stamps etc)* la collezione
(postal) la levata
colour il colore
colour film la pellicola a colori
comb *(noun)* il pettine
(verb) pettinare
come venire
I come from... sono di...
we came last week siamo venuti la settimana scorsa
communication cord il segnale d'allarme
compact disc il compact disc
compartment lo scompartimento
complicated complicato
concert il concerto
conditioner *(hair)* il balsamo
conductor *(bus)* il bigliettaio
(orchestra) il direttore
congratulations! congratulazioni!
constipation la stitichezza
consulate il consolato
contact lenses le lenti a contatto
contraceptive il contraccettivo
cook *(noun)* il cuoco
(verb) cucinare
cooking utensils gli utensili da cucina
cool fresco
cork il tappo
corkscrew il cavatappi
corner l'angolo
corridor il corridoio
Corsica la Corsica
cosmetics i cosmetici
cost *(verb)* costare
what does it cost? quanto costa?
cotton il cotone
cotton wool il cotone idrofilo

cough *(verb)* tossire
(noun) la tosse
council il consiglio
country *(state)* il paese
(not town) la campagna
cousin il cugino
crab il granchio
cramp il crampo
crayfish il gambero
cream *(for cake etc)* la panna
(lotion) la crema
credit card la carta di credito
crew l'equipaggio
crisps le patatine
crowded affollato
cruise la crociera
crutches le stampelle
cry *(weep)* piangere
(shout) il grido
cucumber il cetriolo
cufflinks i gemelli
cup la tazza
cupboard l'armadietto
curlers i bigodini
curls i ricci
curry il curry
curtain la tenda
cut *(noun)* il taglio
(verb) tagliare

dad papà, babbo
dairy *(shop)* la latteria
dark scuro
daughter la figlia
day il giorno
dead morto
deaf sordo
dear *(expensive)* caro, costoso
(cherished) caro
deckchair la sedia a sdraio
deep profondo
deliberately deliberatamente
dentist il dentista
dentures la dentiera
deny: I deny it lo nego
deodorant il deodorante
department store il grande magazzino
departure la partenza
develop *(grow)* svilupparsi
(a film) sviluppare
diamonds *(jewels)* diamanti
(cards) quadri
diarrhoea la diarrea
diary il diario
dictionary il dizionario
die morire
diesel il diesel
different diverso
I'd like a different one ne vorrei un altro
difficult difficile
dining car il vagone ristorante
dining room la sala da pranzo
directory *(telephone)* l'elenco telefonico
dirty sporco
disabled invalido
distributor *(car)* il distributore
dive tuffarsi
diving board il trampolino
divorced divorziato
do fare
doctor il dottore
document il documento
dog il cane
doll la bambola
dollar il dollaro
door la porta
double room una camera doppia
doughnut il krapfen
down giù

drawing pin la puntina da disegno
dress il vestito
drink *(verb)* bere
(noun) la bibita
would you like a drink? vorresti qualcosa da bere?
drinking water l'acqua potabile
drive *(verb: car)* guidare
driver l'autista
driving licence la patente di guida
drunk ubriaco
dry asciutto
(wine) secco
dry cleaner la lavanderia a secco
during durante
dustbin la pattumiera
duster lo straccio per la polvere
Dutch olandese
duty-free il duty free

each ciascuno
(every) ogni
two pounds each due sterline l'uno
early presto
earrings gli orecchini
ears le orecchie
east l'est
easy facile
either: either of them l'uno o l'altro
either... or... o... o...
egg l'uovo
egg cup il portauovo
elastic elastico
elastic band l'elastico
elbows il gomito
electric elettrico
electricity l'elettricità
else: something else qualcos'altro
someone else qualcun'altro
somewhere else da qualche altra parte
embarrassing imbarazzante
embassy l'ambasciata
embroidery il ricamo
emerald lo smeraldo
emergency l'emergenza
empty vuoto
end la fine
engaged *(couple)* fidanzato
(occupied) occupato
engine *(motor)* il motore
(railway) la locomotiva
England l'Inghilterra
English inglese
enlargement l'ampliamento
enough abbastanza
entertainment il divertimento
(show) lo spettacolo
entrance l'entrata
envelope la busta
escalator la scala mobile
especially specialmente
Europe l'Europa
European europeo
evening la sera
every ogni
everyone ognuno, tutti
everything tutto
everywhere dovunque
example l'esempio
for example per esempio
excellent ottimo, eccellente
excess baggage bagaglio in eccesso
exchange *(verb)* scambiare
exchange rate il tasso di cambio
excursion l'escursione
excuse me! mi scusi!

exit l'uscita
expensive caro, costoso
extension lead la prolunga
eye drops le gocce per gli occhi
eyes gli occhi

face la faccia, il viso
faint *(unclear)* indistinto
(verb) svenire
to feel faint sentirsi svenire
fair *(funfair)* il luna park
(just) giusto
it's not fair non è giusto
false teeth la dentiera
fan *(ventilator)* il ventilatore
(enthusiast) l'ammiratore
fan belt la cinghia della ventola
far lontano
fare la tariffa
farm la fattoria
farmer l'agricoltore
fashion la moda
fast veloce
fat grasso
father il padre
feel *(touch)* tastare
I don't feel well non mi sento bene
I feel hot sento caldo
I feel like... ho voglia di...
feet i piedi
felt-tip pen il pennarello
ferry il traghetto
fever la febbre
fiancé il fidanzato
fiancée la fidanzata
field il campo
figs i fichi
filling *(tooth)* la piombatura
(sandwich etc) il ripieno
film il film
finger il dito
fire il fuoco
(blaze) l'incendio
fire extinguisher l'estintore
fireworks i fuochi d'artificio
first primo
first aid il pronto soccorso
first floor il primo piano
fish il pesce
fishing la pesca
to go fishing andare a pesca
fishing rod la canna da pesca
fishmonger il pescivendolo
fizzy frizzante
flag la bandiera
flash *(camera)* il flash
flat *(level)* piatto
(apartment) l'appartamento
flavour il gusto
flight il volo
flip-flops i sandali da spiaggia
flippers le pinne
flour la farina
flower il fiore
flu l'influenza
flute il flauto
fly *(verb)* volare
(insect) la mosca
fog la nebbia
folk music la musica folk
food il cibo
food poisoning un'intossicazione alimentare
foot il piede
football il calcio
for: for me per me
what for? per che cosa?
for a week per una settimana
foreigner lo straniero
forest la foresta
fork la forchetta

fortnight due settimane
fountain pen la penna stilografica
fracture la rottura
France la Francia
free *(no cost)* gratis
(at liberty) libero
freezer il congelatore
French francese
fridge il frigorifero
friend l'amico
friendly cordiale
front: in front davanti
frost il gelo
(on window) il ghiaccio
fruit la frutta
fruit juice il succo di frutta
fry friggere
frying pan la padella
full pieno
I'm full sono sazio
full board la pensione completa
funnel *(for pouring)* l'imbuto
funny divertente
furniture i mobili

garage *(to park car)* il garage
(for repairs) l'autorimessa
garden il giardino
garlic l'aglio
gas-permeable lenses le lenti semi-rigide
gay *(happy)* allegro
(homosexual) omosessuale, gay
gear il cambio
gear lever la leva del cambio
gents *(toilet)* signori
German tedesco
Germany la Germania
get *(fetch)* prendere
have you got...? ha...?
to get the train prendere il treno
get back: we get back tomorrow torniamo domani
get in entrare
(arrive) arrivare
get out uscire
(bring out) tirare fuori
get up *(rise)* alzarsi
gift il regalo
gin il gin
ginger lo zenzero
girl la ragazza
girlfriend la ragazza
give dare
glad contento
I'm glad sono contento
glass *(material)* il vetro
(for drinking) il bicchiere
glasses gli occhiali
gloss prints le fotografie su carta lucida
gloves i guanti
glue la colla
goggles *(skin-diver)* la maschera
(skier) gli occhiali da sci
gold l'oro
good buono
goodbye arrivederci
government il governo
grapes l'uva
grass l'erba
Greece la Grecia
green verde
grey grigio
grill la griglia
grocer *(shop)* il negozio di alimentari
ground floor il pianterreno
ground sheet il telone impermeabile

guarantee *(noun)* la garanzia
(verb) garantire
guard la guardia
(on train) il capotreno
guide book la guida
guitar la chitarra
gun *(rifle)* il fucile
(pistol) la pistola

hair i capelli
hair dryer l'asciugacapelli
hair spray la lacca per i capelli
haircut il taglio (di capelli)
hairdresser il parrucchiere
half metà
half an hour una mezz'ora
half board la mezza pensione
ham il prosciutto
hamburger l'hamburger
hammer il martello
hand la mano
handbag la borsetta
hand brake il freno a mano
handbag la borsetta
handkerchief il fazzoletto
handle *(door)* la maniglia
handsome bello, attraente
hangover i postumi della sbornia
happy felice
harbour il porto
hard duro
hard lenses le lenti dure
hat il cappello
hayfever il raffreddore da fieno
have *(own)* avere
have you got...? ha...?
can I have...? potrei avere...?
I have to go devo andare
he lui
head la testa
headache il mal di testa
headlights i fari
hear udire, sentire
I can't hear you non ti sento
hearing aid l'apparecchio acustico
heart il cuore
(cards) cuori
heart attack l'infarto, l'attacco cardiaco
heating il riscaldamento
heavy pesante
heel il tallone
hello ciao
(to get attention) ehi!
help *(noun)* l'aiuto
(verb) aiutare
help! aiuto!
her: it's her è lei
it's for her è per lei
give it to her daglielo
(possessive) suo, sua
here qui
hers il suo, la sua
high alto
highway code
il codice della strada
hill la collina
him: it's him è lui
it's for him è per lui
give it to him daglielo
his suo, sua
history la storia
hitch hike fare l'autostop
hobby il passatempo, l'hobby
holiday la vacanza
Holland l'Olanda
honest onesto
honey il miele
honeymoon la luna di miele
horn *(car)* il clacson
(animal) il corno

horrible orribile
hospital l'ospedale
hot caldo
hot water bottle
la borsa dell'acqua calda
hour l'ora
house la casa
how? come?
hungry affamato
I'm hungry ho fame
husband il marito

I io
ice il ghiaccio
ice cream il gelato
ice cube il cubetto di ghiaccio
ice lolly il ghiacciolo
ice rink la pista di pattinaggio (sul ghiaccio)
ice-skates i pattini da ghiaccio
if se
ignition l'accensione
immediately immediatamente
impossible impossibile
in: in Rome a Roma
in Italy in Italia
in the room nella camera
India l'India
Indian indiano
indicator *(in station etc)* il tabellone
(of car) la freccia
indigestion la cattiva digestione
infection l'infezione
information le informazioni
injection l'iniezione
injury la ferita, la lesione
ink l'inchiostro
inn la locanda
inner tube la camera d'aria
insect l'insetto
insect repellent l'insettifugo
insomnia l'insonnia
insurance l'assicurazione
interesting interessante
invitation l'invito
Ireland l'Irlanda
Irish irlandese
iron *(metal)* il ferro
(for clothes) il ferro da stiro
ironmonger il negozio di ferramenta
is: he/she/it is è
island l'isola
Italian italiano
Italy l'Italia
itch *(noun)* il prurito
(verb) avere il prurito
my arm itches mi prude il braccio
it itches prude

jacket la giacca
jacuzzi lo jacuzzi
jam la marmellata
jazz il jazz
jealous geloso
jeans i jeans
jellyfish la medusa
jeweller il gioielliere
job il lavoro
jog *(verb)* fare footing
to go for a jog andare a fare footing
joke *(verbal)* la battuta
(practical joke) lo scherzo
journey il viaggio
jumper il maglione
just: it's just arrived è appena arrivato

I've just one left me ne è rimasto solo uno

kettle il bollitore
key la chiave
kidney il rene
kilo il chilo
kilometre il chilometro
kitchen la cucina
knee il ginocchio
knife il coltello
knit lavorare a maglia
knitting needle il ferro (da calza)

label l'etichetta
lace il pizzo
(of shoe) il laccio
ladies *(toilet)* signore
lake il lago
lamb l'agnello
lamp la lampada
lampshade il paralume
land *(noun)* la terra
(verb) atterrare
language la lingua
large grande
last *(final)* ultimo
last week la settimana scorsa
at last! finalmente!
late tardi
it's getting late si sta facendo tardi
the bus is late l'autobus è in ritardo
laugh ridere
launderette la lavanderia (automatica)
laundry *(place)* la lavanderia
(clothes) la biancheria
laxative il lassativo
lazy pigro
leaf *(of plant)* la foglia
(of book) il foglio
learn imparare
leather *(soft)* la pelle
(hard) il cuoio
left *(not right)* sinistra
there's nothing left non c'è rimasto più nulla
left luggage il desposito bagagli
leg la gamba
lemon il limone
lemonade la gazzosa
length la lunghezza
lens la lente
lesson la lezione
letter la lettera
letterbox la cassetta delle lettere
lettuce la lattuga
library la biblioteca
licence *(permit)* l'autorizzazione
(driving) la patente
(trading) la licenza
life la vita
lift *(in building)* l'ascensore
(in car) il passaggio
light *(not heavy)* leggero
(not dark) chiaro
light meter l'esposimetro
lighter l'accendino
lighter fuel il gas
like: I like... mi piace...
what's it like? com'è?
lime *(fruit)* la limetta
lip salve il burro di cacao
lipstick il rossetto
liqueur il liquore
list l'elenco
litre il litro

litter i rifiuti
little *(small)* piccolo
it's a little big è un po' grande
liver il fegato
lobster l'aragosta
lollipop il lecca lecca
lorry il camion
lost property oggetti smarriti
lot: a lot molto
loud forte
(colour) chiassoso
lounge *(in house)* il soggiorno
(in hotel etc) il salone
low basso
luck la fortuna
good luck! buona fortuna!
luggage i bagagli
luggage rack *(train)* la reticella (per i bagagli)
lunch il pranzo

magazine la rivista
mail la posta
make fare
man l'uomo
manager il direttore
map la carta (geografica)
(street map) la pianta
margarine la margarina
market il mercato
marmalade la marmellata d'arance
married sposato
mascara il mascara
mass *(church)* la messa
match *(light)* il fiammifero
(sport) l'incontro, la partita
material *(cloth)* la stoffa
mattress il materasso
maybe forse
me: it's me sono io
it's for me è per me
give it to me dammelo
meal il pasto
meat la carne
mechanic il meccanico
medicine la medicina
Mediterranean il Mediterraneo
meeting l'incontro
melon il melone
menu il menù
message il messaggio
midday mezzogiorno
middle il centro
midnight mezzanotte
milk il latte
mine il mio, la mia
mineral water l'acqua minerale
mirror lo specchio
mistake l'errore
to make a mistake fare un errore
money i soldi
month il mese
monument il monumento
moped il ciclomotore, il motorino
morning la mattina
in the morning la mattina
mother la madre
motorbike la motocicletta
motorboat il motoscafo
motorway l'autostrada
mountain la montagna
moustache i baffi
mouth la bocca
move muovere
much: not much non molto
mug il tazzone
mum mamma
museum il museo
mushrooms i funghi

music la musica
musical instrument lo strumento musicale
musician il musicista
mussels la cozze
mustard la senape
my mio, mia

nail *(metal)* il chiodo
(finger) l'unghia
nail file la limetta per le unghie
nail polish lo smalto per le unghie
narrow stretto
near vicino
near London vicino a Londra
neck il collo
necklace la collana
need *(verb)* avere bisogno di
I need... ho bisogno di...
there's no need non c'e bisogno
needle l'ago
neither: neither of them né l'uno né l'altro
neither... nor... né... né...
negative *(photo)* la negativa
(adj) negativo
nephew il nipote
never mai
new nuovo
New Zealand Nuova Zelanda
news le notizie
newsagent il giornalaio
newspaper il giornale
next prossimo
next week la settimana prossima
what next? e poi?
niece la nipote
night la notte
nightclub il locale notturno, il night
nightdress la camicia da notte
no *(response)* no
(not any) nessuno
noisy rumoroso
north il nord
nose il naso
nose drops le gocce per il naso
not non
notebook il taccuino
novel il romanzo
now ora, adesso
nudist il nudista
number il numero
number plate la targa
nurse l'infermiera
nursery slope la discesa per principianti

occasionally ogni tanto
office l'ufficio
often spesso
oil l'olio
(petroleum) il petrolio
ointment l'unguento
old vecchio
olive l'oliva
omelette la frittata
on: on the table sul tavolo
on Tuesday martedì
on time in orario
onion la cipolla
open *(verb)* aprire
(adj) aperto
operator *(phone)* il centralino
opposite: opposite the theatr di fronte al teatro
optician l'ottico

or o
orange *(colour)* arancione
(fruit) l'arancia
orchestra l'orchestra
organ l'organo
our nostro, nostra
ours il nostro, la nostra
outside fuori
over su
over there laggiù
overtake sorpassare
oyster l'ostrica

pack of cards il mazzo di carte
package *(parcel)* pacco
(smaller) pacchetto
a packet of... un pacchetto di...
page la pagina
pain il dolore
pair il paio
Pakistan il Pakistan
Pakistani Pakistano
pancake la frittella
paracetamol le compresse per il mal di testa
paraffin la paraffina
parcel il pacchetto
pardon? prego?
parents i genitori
park *(noun)* il parco
(verb) parcheggiare
parsley il prezzemolo
party *(celebration)* la festa
(group) il gruppo
passenger il passeggero
passport il passaporto
pasta la pasta
path il sentiero
pay pagare
peach la pesca
peanuts le arachidi
pear la pera
pearl la perla
peas i piselli
pedestrian il pedone
peg *(clothes)* la molletta
pen la penna
pencil la matita
pencil sharpener il temperamatite
penfriend il corrispondente
penknife il temperino
pepper *(& salt)* il pepe
(red/green) il peperone
peppermints la menta piperita
perfume il profumo
perhaps forse
perm la permanente
petrol la benzina
petrol station la stazione di servizio
petticoat la sottoveste
photograph *(noun)* la fotografia
(verb) fotografare
photographer il fotografo
phrase book il vocabolarietto
piano il pianoforte
pickpocket il borsaiolo
picnic il picnic
piece il pezzo
pillow il cuscino
pilot il pilota
pin lo spillo
pineapple l'ananas
pink rosa
pipe *(for smoking)* la pipa
(for water) il tubo
piston *(of car)* il pistone
piston ring la fascia elastica
pizza la pizza
plant la pianta

plaster *(for cut)* il cerotto
plastic la plastica
plastic bag il sacchetto di plastica
plate il piatto
platform il binario
please per favore
plug *(electrical)* la spina
(sink) il tappo
pocket la tasca
poison il veleno
police station la stazione di polizia
policeman il poliziotto
politics la politica
poor povero
(bad quality) di cattiva qualità
pop music la musica pop
pork la carne di maiale
port il porto
porter *(hotel)* il portiere
(station) il facchino
Portugal il Portogallo
post *(noun)* la posta
(verb) spedire per posta
post box la buca delle lettere
post box l'ufficio postale
postcard la cartolina
poster il manifesto
postman il postino
potato la patata
poultry il pollame
pound *(money)* la sterlina
powder la polvere
(cosmetics) la cipria
pram la carrozzina
prawn il gambero
prescription la ricetta
pretty *(beautiful)* grazioso, carino
(quite) piuttosto
priest il prete
private privato
problem il problema
what's the problem? che cosa c'è?
public pubblico
pull tirare
purple viola
purse il borsellino
push spingere
pushchair il passeggino
pyjamas il pigiama

quality la qualità
quay il molo
question la domanda
queue *(noun)* la fila
(verb) fare la fila
quick veloce
quiet tranquillo
quilt la trapunta
quite abbastanza

radiator *(heating)* il radiatore
radio la radio
radish il ravanello
railway line la linea ferroviaria
rain la pioggia
raincoat l'impermeabile
raisin l'uva passa
rare *(uncommon)* raro
(steak) al sangue
raspberry il lampone
razor blades le lamette
reading lamp la lampada da studio
ready pronto
rear lights i fari posteriori
receipt la ricevuta
receptionist il/la receptionist

record *(music)* il disco
record player il giradischi
record shop il negozio di dischi
red rosso
refreshments i rinfreschi
registered letter l'assicurata
relax rilassarsi
religion la religione
remember ricordare
reservation la prenotazione
rest *(remainder)* il resto
(relax) riposarsi
restaurant il ristorante
restaurant car il vagone ristorante
return *(come back)* tornare
(give back) restituire
rice il riso
rich ricco
right *(correct)* giusto, esatto
(direction) destro
ring *(to call)* telefonare
(wedding etc) l'anello
ripe maturo
river il fiume
road la strada
rock *(stone)* la roccia
(music) il rock
roll *(bread)* il panino
(verb) rotolare
roller skates i pattini a rotelle
room la stanza
(space) lo spazio
rope la corda
rose la rosa
round *(circular)* rotondo
it's my round tocca a me offrire
rowing boat la barca a remi
rubber *(eraser)* la gomma
rubbish l'immondizie
ruby *(colour)* color rubino
rucksack lo zaino
rug *(mat)* il tappeto
(blanket) il plaid
ruins le rovine, i resti
ruler la riga
rum il rum
runway la pista

sad triste
safe sicuro
safety pin la spilla di sicurezza
sailing boat la barca a vela
salad l'insalata
salami il salame
sale la vendita
(at reduced prices) la svendita, i saldi
salmon il salmone
salt il sale
same stesso
sand la sabbia
sand dunes le dune
sandals i sandali
sandwich il panino
sanitary towels gli assorbenti (igienici)
sauce la salsa
saucepan la pentola
sauna la sauna
sausage la salsiccia
say: what did you say? che ha detto?
how do you say...? come si dice...?
scampi gli scampi
Scandinavia la Scandinavia
scarf la sciarpa
school la scuola
scissors le forbici
Scotland la Scozia

Scottish scozzese
screw la vite
screwdriver il cacciavite
sea il mare
seat il posto
seat belt la cintura di sicurezza
see vedere
I can't see non vedo
I see! capisco!
sell vendere
sellotape ® lo scotch ®
serious serio
serviette il tovagliolo
several parecchi, diversi
sew cucire
shampoo lo shampoo
shave: to have a shave farsi la barba
shaving foam la schiuma da barba
shawl lo scialle
she lei
sheet il lenzuolo
shell la conchiglia
sherry lo sherry
ship la nave
shirt la camicia
shoe laces i lacci per le scarpe
shoe polish il lucido per le scarpe
shoe shop la calzoleria
shoes le scarpe
shop il negozio
shopping la spesa
to go shopping andare a fare la spesa
shopping centre il centro commerciale
short corto
shorts gli shorts, i calzoncini
shoulder la spalla
shower *(bath)* la doccia
(rain) l'acquazzone
shrimp il gamberetto
shutter *(camera)* l'otturatore
(window) l'imposta
Sicily la Sicilia
sick *(ill)* malato
I feel sick ho la nausea
side *(edge)* il lato
(page) la facciata
I'm on his side sono dalla sua parte
sidelights le luci di posizione
silk la seta
silver *(colour)* argenteo
(metal) l'argento
simple semplice
sing cantare
single *(one)* solo
(unmarried man) celibe
(unmarried woman) nubile
single room la camera singola
sister la sorella
skates i pattini
ski *(noun)* lo sci
(verb) sciare
to go skiing andare a sciare
ski stick la racchetta (da sci)
ski-lift la seggiovia
skid *(verb)* slittare
skin cleanser il latte detergente
skirt la gonna
sky il cielo
sledge la slitta
sleep *(noun)* il sonno
(verb) dormire
to go to sleep addormentarsi
sleeping bag il sacco a pelo
sleeping car il vagone letto
sleeping pill il sonnifero
sling *(medical)* la fascia
slippers le pantofole
slow lento

small piccolo
smell *(noun)* l'odore
(stench) il puzzo
(verb) sentire odore di
I smell burning sento odore di bruciato
smile *(noun)* il sorriso
(verb) sorridere
smoke *(noun)* il fumo
(verb) fumare
snack lo spuntino
snorkel il respiratore a tubo
snow la neve
so così
soaking solution *(for contact lenses)* il liquido per lenti
soap il sapone
socks i calzini
soda water l'acqua di seltz
soft lenses le lenti morbide
somebody qualcuno
somehow in qualche modo
something qualcosa
sometimes qualche volta, a volte
somewhere da qualche parte
son il figlio
song la canzone
sorry: I'm sorry mi scusi
soup la zuppa
south il sud
souvenir il souvenir
spade *(shovel)* la vanga
(cards) picche
Spain la Spagna
Spanish spagnolo
spanner la chiave fissa
spares i pezzi di ricambio
spark(ing) plug la candela
speak parlare
do you speak...? parla...?
I don't speak... non parlo...
speed la velocità
speedometer il tachimetro
spider il ragno
spinach gli spinaci
spoon il cucchiaio
sprain la slogatura
spring *(mechanical)* la molla
(season) la primavera
stadium lo stadio
staircase la scala
stairs le scale
stamp il francobollo
stapler la cucitrice
star la stella
(film) il divo
start l'inizio
(in race) la partenza
station la stazione
statue la statua
steak la bistecca
steamer la nave a vapore
steering wheel il volante
steward lo steward
sting *(noun)* la puntura
(verb) pungere
it stings brucia
stockings le calze
stomach lo stomaco
stomach-ache il mal di stomaco
stop *(verb)* fermare
the bus stopped l'autobus si è fermato
(cease) smettere di
bus stop la fermata dell'autobus
stop! alt!
storm la tempesta
strawberry la fragola
stream *(small river)* il ruscello
string *(cord)* lo spago
(guitar etc) la corda
student lo studente
stupid stupido

suburbs la periferia
sugar lo zucchero
suit *(noun)* il completo
(verb) adattare
it suits you ti sta bene
suit yourself! fa' come ti pare!
suitcase la valigia
sun il sole
sunbathe prendere il sole
sunburn la scottatura
sunglasses gli occhiali da sole
sunny assolato
a sunny day una giornata di sole
suntan l'abbronzatura
suntan lotion la lozione solare
supermarket il supermercato
supplement il supplemento
sweat *(verb)* sudare
(noun) il sudore
sweatshirt il maglione in cotone felpato
sweet *(not sour)* dolce
(candy) la caramella
swimming costume il costume da bagno
swimming pool la piscina
swimming trunks il costume da bagno (per uomo)
switch l'interruttore
synagogue sinagoga

table il tavolo
tablet la compressa
take prendere
take-off *(noun)* il decollo
(verb) decollare
take-away portar via
take-away pizzas pizze da portar via

talcum powder il talco
talk parlare
(noun) la conversazione
tall alto
tampon il tampone
tangerine il mandarino
tap il rubinetto
tapestry l'arazzo
tea il tè
tea towel lo strofinaccio
telegram il telegramma
telephone *(noun)* il telefono
(verb) telefonare
telephone box la cabina telefonica
telephone call la telefonata
television la televisione
temperature *(heat)* la temperatura
(fever) la febbre
tent la tenda
tent peg il picchetto *(da tenda)*
tent pole il palo della tenda
than di
thank *(verb)* ringraziare
thanks grazie
thank you very much grazie mille
that: that man quell'uomo
that woman quella donna
what's that? cos'è quello?
I think that... penso che...
their loro
theirs il loro, la loro
them: it's them sono loro
it's for them è per loro
give it to them dallo a loro
then poi, allora
there lì
thermos flask il thermos
these: these things queste cose
these are mine queste sono le mi

hey loro, essi
hick spesso
hin sottile
hink pensare
I think so penso di sì
I'll think about it ci penserò
hirsty assetato
I'm thirsty ho sete
his: this man quest'uomo
this woman questa donna
what's this? cos'è questo?
hose: those things quelle cose
those are his quelle sono le sue
hroat la gola
hroat pastilles le pasticche per la gola
hrough attraverso
hunderstorm il temporale
icket il biglietto
ide la marea
ie *(noun)* la cravatta
(verb) legare
ime il tempo
what's the time? che ore sono?
imetable l'orario
in la scatola
in opener l'apriscatola
ip *(money)* la mancia
(end) la punta
ired stanco
I feel tired sono stanco
issues i fazzolettini di carta
o: to the station alla stazione
to England in Inghilterra
oast il pane tostato
obacco il tabacco
oboggan il toboga
oday oggi
ogether insieme
oilet la toilette
toilet paper la carta igienica
tomato il pomodoro
tomorrow domani
tongue la lingua
tonic l'acqua tonica
tonight stasera
too *(also)* anche
(excessive) troppo
toothache il mal di denti
tooth il dente
toothbrush lo spazzolino da denti
toothpaste il dentifricio
torch la torcia elettrica
tour il giro
(of building) la visita
tourist il turista
towel l'asciugamano
tower la torre
town la città
town hall il municipio
toy il giocattolo
toy shop il negozio di giocattoli
track suit la tuta da ginnastica
tractor il trattore
tradition la tradizione
traffic il traffico
traffic lights il semaforo
trailer il rimorchio
train il treno
translate tradurre
transmission la trasmissione
travel agency l'agenzia di viaggio
traveller's cheque il traveller's chèque
tray il vassoio
tree l'albero
trousers i pantaloni
try provare
tunnel la galleria, il tunnel
tweezers le pinzette

typewriter la macchina da scrivere
tyre la gomma

umbrella l'ombrello
uncle lo zio
under sotto
underground la metropolitana
underpants le mutande
unmarried *(man)* celibe
(woman) nubile
university l'università
until fino a
unusual insolito
up su
(upwards) verso l'alto
urgent urgente
us: it's us siamo noi
it's for us è per noi
give it to us daccelo
use *(noun)* l'uso
(verb) usare
it's no use non serve a niente
useful utile
usual solito
usually di solito

vacancy una stanza libera
vacuum cleaner l'aspirapolvere
vacuum flask il thermos
valley la valle
valve la valvola
vanilla la vaniglia
vase il vaso
veal la carne di vitello
vegetables la verdura
vegetarian *(person)* il vegetariano
vehicle il veicolo
very molto
vest la maglietta intima
view la vista
viewfinder il mirino
villa la villa
village il villaggio
vinegar l'aceto
violin il violino
visa il visto
visit *(noun)* la visita
(verb) andare a trovare
visitor l'ospite
(tourist) il turista
vitamin tablet la compressa di vitamine
vodka la vodka
voice la voce

wait aspettare
waiter il cameriere
waiting room la sala d'attesa
waitress la cameriera
Wales il Galles
walk *(verb)* camminare
(noun) la passeggiata
to go for a walk andare a fare una passeggiata
walkman ® il walkman
wall *(inside)* la parete
(outside) il muro
wallet il portafoglio
war la guerra
wardrobe il guardaroba
warm caldo
was: I was ero
he/she/it was era
washing powder il detersivo (per bucato)
washing-up liquid il detersivo liquido per piatti
wasp la vespa

watch *(noun)* l'orologio
(verb) guardare
water l'acqua
waterfall la cascata
wave *(noun)* l'onda
(verb) salutare
we noi
weather il tempo
wedding il matrimonio
week la settimana
wellingtons gli stivali di gomma
Welsh gallese
were: we were eravamo
they were erano
you were *(singular familiar)* eri
(singular polite) Lei era
(plural familiar) eravate
(plural polite) Loro erano
west l'ovest
wet bagnato
vhat? cosa?
what is it? che cos'è?
vheel la ruota
vheelchair la sedia a rotelle
vhen? quando?
vhere? dove?
vhether se
vhich? quale?
vhisky il whisky
vhite bianco
vho? chi?
vhy? perché?
vide ampio
vife la moglie
vind il vento
vindow la finestra
vindscreen il parabrezza
vindscreen wiper il tergicristallo
vine il vino
vine list la lista dei vini
vine merchant il negozio di vini
wing l'ala
with con
without senza
woman la donna
wood *(forest)* il bosco
(material) il legno
wool la lana
word la parola
work *(noun)* il lavoro
(verb) lavorare
(machine etc) funzionare
worse peggio
wrapping paper la carta da imballaggio
(for presents) la carta da regalo
wrist il polso
writing paper la carta da scrivere
wrong sbagliato

year l'anno
yellow giallo
yes sì
yesterday ieri
yet: is it ready yet? è pronto?
not yet non ancora
yoghurt lo yogurt
you: *(singular familiar* tu
(singular polite) Lei
(plural familiar) voi
(plural polite) Loro
your: *(singular familiar)* tuo, tua
(singular polite) Suo, Sua
(plural familiar) vostro, vostra
(plural polite) Loro
youth hostel l'ostello della gioventù
Yugoslavia la Jugoslavia
zip la chiusura lampo
zoo lo zoo